THE SONS OF BARDSTOWN

THE SONS OF BARDSTOWN

25 Years
of Vietnam
in an
American
Town

JIM WILSON

CROWN PUBLISHERS, INC.   NEW YORK

Published by Crown Publishers, Inc., 201 East 50th Street, New York, New York 10022. Member of the Crown Publishing Group.

Random House, Inc. New York, Toronto, London, Sydney, Auckland

CROWN is a trademark of Crown Publishers, Inc.

Manufactured in the United States of America

Book design by June Bennett-Tantillo

Library of Congress Cataloging-in-Publication Data
Wilson, Jim
The sons of Bardstown / by Jim Wilson.—1st ed.
p. cm.
Includes index.
1. Vietnamese Conflict, 1961–1975—United States. 2. Bardstown (Ky.)—History. I. Title.
DS558.W55 1994
959.704′3373—dc20   93-31576
CIP

ISBN 0-517-57737-2

10 9 8 7 6 5 4 3 2 1

First Edition

To Mrs. Dixie Hibbs
and the people of Bardstown

Contents

THE SONS OF BARDSTOWN

Introduction

Bardstown didn't need the war in Vietnam to put it on the map. It was already there, and had been for 185 years, ever since the spring of 1780, when three hundred restless adventurers drifted down what is now the Ohio River in search of a new life. The East was too crowded, they felt, and they had heard of a distant land where there was still plenty of room for a man to put up a cabin and raise a family without bumping into a neighbor every day or so. Many were single men. A few had families. Each packed his few belongings and headed west. Days later, they poled their way to shore at a place called the Falls of the Ohio.

The water there was too rough to navigate, the rocks far too dangerous to challenge, so they splashed ashore and began to portage around the Falls, an area that later became known as Louisville, in a land called Kentucky by the Indians and early settlers. They didn't get too far before they ran into William Bard, certainly one of the country's first land developers. He told them of a new town that he was planning on Stewart's Creek, about thirty-five miles southeast of the Falls on a thousand-acre land claim he had made for his brother, David, and John C. Owings, an ironmonger from Baltimore, Maryland.

William Bard, agent for brother David and Owings, told the settlers that he was authorized to "divide a town that was to be called Salem." He told them that he would sell town lots, and in

August 1780, he held a lottery to divide the original thirty-three lots in what for a very brief time was called Salem.

William and David Bard were raised in nearby Pennsylvania, in an area that is now Adams County. Later, they moved to the western part of the state, then to Kentucky.

In the late 1700s, Fort Pitt was the jumping-off point for travel down the Ohio River toward the western frontier, toward Kentucky. The Bards were adventurers, scouts, explorers; William more so than his younger brother, David. There was a lot of land out there, on the far side of the Appalachians, and all you had to do to claim it was put your mark on a few trees. William Bard crossed the mountains into Kentucky in 1775 or 1776 looking for salt, built a tiny cabin, spent a few weeks there, then returned to Pennsylvania, to the Fort Pitt area.

"It was very dangerous, almost foolhardy, to go out there," says historian David H. Hall.

It was a big gamble for several reasons, but a lot of people took it. You could lose your scalp. After you staked your claim, you eventually had to pay the Colonial government at Williamsburg, Virginia, a fee based on the size of your claim, and few pioneers had any money. And no settler could be sure that Virginia would approve the claim, because there was a treaty with the Indians signed before the Revolution began that specified that settlers could not cross the Appalachians to settle permanently on Indian lands.

The Bards had the land, but no money to pay for it. Owings, who had an ironworks in Baltimore, had just received a large sum in notes of paper money from Virginia for services rendered in the Revolution. The catch was that its greatest value was in the exchange-purchase of virgin land in the Kentucky wilderness just opening up because of new Virginia laws. David Bard got the money he needed for land warrants from Owings and in return agreed to split everything down the middle with the ironmonger. Then they named William Bard, who had made the claim, to be their land agent on the frontier, to establish the town and to monitor its early affairs.

By the time the settlers had arrived at the Falls of the Ohio, the entire region had already acquired a very bad reputation. Along the western frontier, it was known as a land where various tribes went to hunt game, settle their disputes, and raid the cabins of a few very early settlers who had foolishly moved too far from civilization in 1774 or 1775. Many of these were enticed to Kentucky, which at that time was part of Virginia, by the Colonial powers at Williamsburg, who promised all settlers four hundred acres of land, free, if they would go out there, face the Indians, and stay long enough to harvest one crop of corn. Some made it. Many didn't. The Falls itself wasn't a safe place to be, either, because in addition to the Indians, there were diseases and gangs of riverboat roughnecks who preyed on the early pioneers going down the river. In fact, just about all of Kentucky was known as the "dark and bloody ground."

Indians had always been in the area, probably going back as far as twenty-five thousand years. Early explorers, such as England's Col. Abram Wood, Gabriel Arthur, and John Peter Salley, and France's Fathers Jacques Marquette and Louis Joliet, found Delaware, Cherokee, Iroquois, and Shawnee there in the late 1600s and the early 1700s. Kentucky got its name from an old Cherokee word that loosely means "Land of Tomorrow" and "Meadowland." In 1750, pioneer scout Thomas Walker became the first white man to fully explore the region. Daniel Boone got his first glimpse of the promised land in 1767, and liked what he saw. So he went back two years later, but the Indians drove him out. He returned in 1773 with a few dozen settlers, but his party was too few, the Indians too many, and he was forced out a second time. He went back to stay in 1775, building a frontier outpost called Boonesboro, which later became a town. The oldest town in Kentucky is Harrodsburg, founded in 1774.

This was wild country. One could run around in there for weeks, months, and never see or be seen by another human being.

Once the town lots were drawn at Spring Station on Bear Grass Creek, a short distance from present-day Louisville, some of the settlers followed Bard to the town site. Others went there later. Some sold their lots on the spot for an immediate profit. And others simply lost their land because they never made improvements necessary to retain their lots, such as clearing brush and building a shelter with sixteen square feet of floor space with a roof.

Most of these settlers were searching for a stake in life. Their families were back east, where the Revolutionary War was raging, and at this time, no one had any idea which side would win. These early pioneers felt that if they found fertile land on the far side of the mountains, they would be far enough away so that it didn't matter who won, the British or the Americans.

No money changed hands between Bard and the settlers. He told them that title to the land would be worked out after the Indian problems were resolved. Bard showed each settler where his lot was and explained how the town would be laid out, where the streets would run: it would be a grid pattern, similar to Philadelphia.

This was land speculation in its purest sense on the part of Bard. If the town grew and prospered, then the other sixty-three lots he had there would jump in value. So would the value of the wild and ominous land that surrounded the town, and Bard held much of that.

The original town was three and one-half blocks long by four and one-half blocks wide. There were two acres to a block and eight lots in a block. Since the town was on a plateau, the drainage was good, and in the long, hot summers, wind usually kept the area cool. Property lines inside the town were precise. The first map of the town, drawn by John Filson in 1784, clearly showed the location of each lot. The big problems arose when other settlers tried to determine who owned what land outside the town. It was impossible to determine where one man's land ended and another man's land began. Descriptions were vague. "Go up the creek to the big sycamore . . ." "When you pass the three large stones, go west . . ." Surveys were made according to the contour of the land, where ridges, streams, valleys, and tree lines ran. Lawyers were kept busy with claims and counterclaims in the countryside, trying to untangle the tangled property lines. So were surveyors. It wasn't until around 1830 that these land claims were straightened out. Yet to this day, there are bits and pieces of land, a half acre here, two acres there, that belong to no one, land whose property lines never did correspond with another property line.

Another problem was the great distances along the frontier. Because of this, the region was virtually ungovernable from faraway Virginia. It was a three-week ride on horseback to reach Williamsburg by those living on the frontier if they wanted a say in how they were to be governed. More important, the great distance made it impossible for Virginia to defend the early settlers from the Indians. Although the new Bardstown settlement was not a fortified town, there were fortified "safe houses" scattered about so that in time of great danger, the families could take shelter there.

There was but one thing to do—petition Virginia for separate statehood, and hope for the best. Surprisingly, the "best" came in 1792, when Kentucky became the fifteenth state.

The entire region around Bard's new town had been named Nelson County in 1784 by the Virginia House of Burgesses to honor a former governor of Virginia, Thomas Nelson. The area was so large that it was later divided into twenty-four other counties.

The first public buildings went up in 1784–85, including a log courthouse and a jail. In 1790, the log courthouse was replaced by a Georgian-style edifice made of limestone in the center of town, where gifted orators, including Henry Clay, later spoke.

Very few of the early settlers called the new town by its designated name, Salem. Most called it either "Bard's Town" or "Baird's Town," the latter a reference to James Baird, another pioneer who moved his family west from Pennsylvania to the new settlement in Kentucky, according to historian Hall. Although separate families, the Bards and the Bairds were tenuously connected by a marriage of in-laws years earlier in Pennsylvania. In other words, they knew each other, Hall said. Most of the early settlers in the region were of Scotch-Irish descent. When one of them referred to the new town, it was impossible to determine if that individual was saying "Bard," "Baird," or even "Beard." There was no way one could determine the correct spelling. Young clerks, inexperienced, careless, spelled the name of the town both ways—"Bard's Town" and "Baird's Town"—on early town documents, according to Hall. It was spelled both ways on records in Virginia. On Filson's map of the area in 1784, it was spelled "Bard's Town." On later maps it was sometimes spelled "Baird's Town." It wasn't until 1815 that the spelling was changed to "Bardstown," which it is today. A few years after the town was settled, about 1784–85, William Bard moved his family to Danville, Kentucky, about thirty miles away, and seldom returned. The rest of the Bairds remained in Bardstown and until the 1790s were a force in the area.

Corn was the basic crop in those early days, simply because it required so little care and attention and fed both man and beast. The earth was so rich that all one had to do was drop a seed and watch it grow. So one planted corn in the spring, stayed close to the cabin or went into a safe house or a stockade, if there was one close by, then harvested the crop in the fall. Corn, in addition to being a large part of the diet then, was used to barter.

Bardstown was a new stopping-off point on the way west, offering unlimited opportunities to those who wanted to settle there, and so it prospered. By 1790, there were more people living in Bardstown than in Louisville. After the War of 1812, the frontier began to move west again, and Bardstown was left behind as the restless young sought out new horizons. Corn remained the primary crop in the early 1800s. It grew so well that the farmers didn't know what to do with it all. A lot was shipped downriver on the Ohio to the Mississippi to New Orleans. But much of it spoiled on the long journey.

The farmers had to turn that excess corn into something that would not spoil. Many of the early settlers here, with roots in nearby Pennsylvania, brought with them a basic knowledge of whiskey-making, using various grains, including rye, as the primary ingredients. Why not make whiskey using corn as the primary ingredient? They tried it, liked it, and a new industry was born. Back then, the whiskey was made mostly with corn, a little rye and barley, and a bit of yeast to make it ferment. It was aged in white oak barrels for six months, at most. Several years later, the warehouse in Bourbon County where the barrels were stored was destroyed by fire. Many of the barrels were burned. Many others were charred on the inside. Nevertheless, the owner decided to store the whiskey in the barrels that were charred. Later, when the whiskey from the charred barrels was tasted, many people found it much better than the whiskey that came from barrels that were not charred.

"Say, did you taste that whiskey from Bourbon County?" townspeople asked each other. A few years later, the whiskey was just called "Bourbon." Elija Craig, a Baptist, is credited with making the first bourbon. Bourbon County is northeast of Lexington and about ninety miles from Nelson County. There has always been a strong French influence in Kentucky dating back to its earliest days. Bourbon County acquired its name from the House of Bourbon, founded in 1272 that produced the rulers of France from 1589 to 1793, and again from 1814 to 1830.

At first, the whiskey was made in small batches. Farmers drank some and used some as trade material and as a form of money. It quickly caught on, and the batches grew in size. Different families developed quite distinctive ways of making it, so the taste varied from one producer to another.

Bourbon today is distilled from fermented mash consisting of not less than fifty-one percent corn grain. Add barley, rye, and a little malt to the corn, grind the mixture into meal, add water, and cook. The mixture is cooled and pumped into large vats. The addition of yeast creates alcohol through the fermentation of the starches and sugars in the grain. This takes about seventy-two hours. The fermented mash is then pumped into stills and heated, and the alcohol comes off as a vapor. This vapor is cooled, condenses, and flows from the tail end of the still, clear as water. This is the way bourbon has been produced since around 1912.

Today, most bourbons are aged four, six, or eight years, still in white oak barrels charred on the inside. This charring caramelizes the wood sugar in the barrels. The wood soaks up the bourbon in the winter, and the hot summers force it out. Going into and out of the wood gives bourbon its color. The barrels are used once, then sold.

"It's a lot like using a tea bag. The second time around, it's not the same," explains Dixie Hibbs, who has written a book on the history of Bardstown and Nelson County.

As time passed and the rest of the country continued west to see what was on the other side of the next mountain, Bardstown settled into a period of slow but steady growth, in stature if not in size, and became a center for education, medicine, law, religion, commerce, and crafts.

The first settlers in the area were mostly Presbyterians and Baptists. There were only two or three Catholic families back then. But between 1780 and 1790, seventy-five Catholic families moved into the area from Maryland. They were farmers; their land in Maryland was worn out and wasn't worth leaving to their sons. So they moved to the southern part of Nelson County, which at that time was one-sixth the size of present-day Kentucky.

A few of the locations where Catholic families from St. Mary's County in southern Maryland settled prior to 1800 were Pottinger Creek, Hardin Creek, Bardstown, Cartwright's Creek, Rolling Fork, Cox's Creek, and Breckenridge. The Pottinger Creek settlement was begun in 1785, a few miles from where present-day Boston is located in Nelson County.

The land in Kentucky then was rich and fertile. But apparently there was one exception—Pottinger Creek. The poor soil at that location led to a tradition that was described by J. Edwin Coad in an article that was reprinted in an 1897 issue of a publication in Maryland called the *St. Mary's Beacon*.

> When I was a boy, there was a tradition rife here to the effect that when the old pioneers from this section used to meet Saturday evenings in Bardstown as soon as they had shaken hands, one would turn his back to the other and beg him for a half dozen kicks under his coat-tail and when they were duly administered, the other would turn around and ask his friend for his kicking. . . . Why was this done, you ask? Why, in order to get temporal punishment inflicted, to expiate the grievous sin they had committed in abandoning the peaceful shores of Maryland for (the poor soil and) the wild forests and savage Indians of Kentucky. But the plunge had been made, the labor and exposure of going forbade the idea of return, and it was a clear case of "root hog or die" . . .

Salem Academy opened in 1787 and started a long tradition of quality education in the area. Rome made Bardstown a diocese in 1808, at the same time as Boston, Philadelphia, and New York. St. Joseph's Cathedral, the first west of the Appalachians, which stretch from Quebec to Alabama, was built by a French priest, Father Benedict Joseph Flaget, the first bishop of Bardstown. Bishop Flaget arrived in the area in 1810 and lived on land close to Bardstown that was donated to the church by a Catholic family whose name was Thomas. The first residence and seminary were built there. Today, St. Thomas Church stands on the site. In 1815,

Bishop Flaget moved to Bardstown and began building St. Joseph's Cathedral, which took about four years. When Bishop Flaget ran into trouble, it was the Protestants who came to his aid in order to complete the cathedral in the wilderness. In 1841, the see was moved to fast-growing Louisville, and St. Joseph's continued as a parish church; today, it is called a protocathedral, meaning either the first, foremost, or earliest cathedral.

St. Joseph's College opened its doors in 1820 and began the teaching of Latin and Greek in an atmosphere that attracted educators and those seeking an education.

Later, St. Joseph's closed its doors, and an orphanage took over the location from 1890 through 1910. Then, in 1911, the Xaverian Brothers reopened the doors under the name of St. Joseph's Preparatory School. They were good teachers. If you wanted a good education, it was there. But they were strict, too. There were rules for everything, and the brothers brooked no nonsense. If you were out of line, they didn't hesitate to knock you back in line. A number of the students were the spoiled, pampered sons of the rich, who had been kicked out of schools elsewhere, whose parents wanted them to get the discipline they were not getting at home. Others went there to get a quality education. For one reason or another, young men from all over the country showed up at St. Joe's Prep, until it closed its doors in 1968 because of declining enrollment.

Most of the girls in town during the fifties and sixties dated the boys at St. Joe's rather than local boys.

"I dated mostly the boys there because they seemed a little more worldly and they could tell me what went on outside Bardstown," says Bobbie Brown, who runs her family's motel in Bardstown. "I had never been anyplace except Louisville, and I was very interested in getting away from Bardstown and seeing what the rest of the world had to offer.

"We used to have dances in the basement of our restaurant next door, but they were always chaperoned," she adds. "Everyone would bring their records, we'd turn the jukebox on and dance." Sometimes some of the boys would sneak off campus to attend.

"Then we'd get a phone call that one of the brothers had discovered their absence, and they'd scatter in all directions trying to get back without being caught. Usually, they were caught," Bobbie remembers.

The Bardstown bar was as full of talent as any in the Kentucky region, and many of its lawyers were becoming known throughout the country.

Pioneer physicians Ephraim McDowell and Walter Brashear studied and practiced here amid a healthy medical climate that led to the first successful amputation of a leg at the hip by Brashear.

Bardstown's craftsmen were second to none, turning out ornate silver jewelry, delicate timepieces, surveying instruments, quality firearms, and fancy leather riding boots, shoes, and saddles. Jacob Rizer, one of the finest gunsmiths of his time, practiced his trade here.

Merchants bought and sold goods that were shipped throughout the country. Great amounts of hemp were grown, turned into rope, and sold to customers in Natchez and New Orleans. Big warehouses began to appear.

Then the plain, drab homes began to take on a new look, that of elegance. Second and third floors were added. It took years to finish some of them. It was almost like "can you top this," with each family trying to outdo the other.

After the Civil War, the whiskey industry began to grow as the railroads opened the West. By 1896, whiskey was the unquestioned king of the hill in Nelson County, and it flowed in ever-increasing quantities from twenty-two distilleries, thanks mostly to the Presbyterians and Baptists who were instrumental in the whiskey-making business around Bardstown. The making of whiskey knew no religious boundaries. Everyone had a hand in it. Some hands were just larger than others, such as those of the Beam family, one of the historic distillers here around 1785. "Back then, everyone made distilled spirits," historian Hall recalls. "A lot of the people had small stills they could carry on horseback. Before they were making whiskey, they were making brandy from fermented peaches.

"They all felt they had a right to make whiskey, just as they had a right to kill hogs or grow corn," Hall adds.

While the whiskey business was flourishing legally in the late nineteenth and early twentieth centuries, the illegal making of whiskey—known as "moonshine" or "white lightning"—was growing by leaps and bounds deep in the hills where strangers were not tolerated and very often shot. Stills were everywhere. Millions of gallons of raw whiskey were made by cooking the mash at night—by the shine of the moon—for if it was done during the day, the "revenooers" would surely have spotted the smoke rising above the trees. Today, most illegal stills are found by tracing the leftover mash that runs into streams and creeks. Legal or illegal, it made no difference. Whiskey is what the people wanted, and whiskey is what they got. The production of bourbon was the top money-maker in these parts for years, and very definitely the area's major industry, until Prohibition brought the business to its knees in 1920. The government swiftly padlocked all the distilleries and put the workers out on the street. So they took the know-how they had acquired working in the distilleries and went up into the hills and put it to use for themselves making moonshine.

The distillers had so much whiskey in their warehouses that the government relented, somewhat, and allowed it to be sold under the guise of "medicinal spirits." The distillers sold the whiskey to brokers, who in turn sold it to drugstores. The original distillery labels were still on the bottles. Drugstores simply added another label advertising the contents as "Medicinal Spirits." Regardless of what you called the contents, the bottles could be only sold by a doctor's prescription. So doctors kept writing prescriptions, and the people kept taking them to the drugstores until all the whiskey was sold, which took several years.

When Prohibition was repealed in 1933, fourteen distilleries opened over a two-year period, and Bardstown slowly returned to the whiskey business. It wasn't until 1937 that the first bourbon was sold again, because it had to age a minimum of four years. Today, four distilleries—Maker's Mark, Jim Beam, Heaven Hill, and Barton Brands—produce more bourbon than did the twenty-two distilleries before the turn of the century.

"At night, when there's a slight breeze, you can smell the mash cooking," says Dixie Hibbs. "It's wonderful!"

People in these parts have always had a different view toward the making of whiskey, moonshine, Prohibition, the law. "We've been doing this all our lives, and taking our livelihood away, well, we felt we were not breaking the law. We felt the law was wrong, not us," she explains.

Any way you look at it, the people of Bardstown feel they have a nice place to raise a family. It's friendly. "Just far enough south to enjoy the hospitality, and far enough north that you don't get grits with every meal," Dixie Hibbs says. Over the years, the people have retained much of what they cherished most—a pleasant, slow pace, the charm that goes with living in an almost model small, close-knit town where values are shaped by the customs and traditions that go with coming of age in a community whose population was but 5,273 in 1965, when the fighting in Vietnam began to move into high gear. Living in a town like this, whose boundaries stretch a bit over a mile in any direction from the town square, is a lot like living in a small fish bowl. Everyone sees you, knows what you are doing at all times. It's as though you are part of one large family, with all the positive and negative aspects of its closeness. You went with his sister. She dated your older brother. Everyone is connected in one way or another, particularly when tragedy strikes, because when one hurts, everyone hurts.

"Just say something bad about someone, and you'll find out who's kin to who," a diner in Hurst's Restaurant remarks.

Back in the sixties, there were no strangers in Bardstown.

"I liked it that way," says Mrs. Joy Janes, who has lived here all her life. "When you went downtown, everyone you saw, you knew." Doors were never locked. Nor were cars. People simply didn't tamper with another person's belongings. You could walk at night and not worry. There was no pollution, no violence, very little crime, and even less drugs. The biggest problem the police had was catching the drag racers on the back roads. If you ordered a sandwich and asked for a cup of coffee, you didn't pay extra for the coffee. And you never saw Christmas decorations anywhere in town until the day after Thanksgiving. For decades, this was Bardstown.

If there was a "hangout" in Bardstown over the years, it must have been the "Old Yellow Corner" on Courthouse Square, where the drugstore is today. For years, women met there in the morning, young people gathered there after school, and their fathers showed up in the evening to talk politics, crops, and sports, or to swap rumors. In the town's very early years, one of its wealthiest residents had been John Caldwell, who was as eccentric as he was rich. Over the years, though, he lost most of his fortune, until all that was left was the old rickety building on the northwest corner of the square, where he lived. It was always painted a dull yellow—thus the sobriquet, the "Old Yellow Corner." Caldwell seldom spoke to anyone, almost never ventured out, and kept a coffin in his room for use when he passed away, which happened in 1846. Then the building changed hands.

During the Civil War, when Federal troops occupied Bardstown, the cellar of the "Yellow Corner" was used as a jail to hold southern sympathizers. Then it was used as a drugstore, first by A. J. Mattingly, then by James Wilson. The old building was torn down, and a new structure, one of yellow brick, was erected in its place. No one seems to know if yellow brick was selected by accident or if it was intentional. A Frenchman, John Losson, had the "Yellow Corner" next, and for four years, it was a restaurant. A German, whose name history seems to have misplaced, got the "Yellow Corner" after that, and again it became a drugstore. A few years later, the location again changed hands when J. Dan Talbott, another druggist, took over and held the "Yellow Corner" until the mid-1930s, when another German immigrant and druggist, John Ed Willmes, set up shop there. The soda fountain ran across the front of the store, and there were five booths down the center. He ran a tight ship, patrolling the aisles like a drill sergeant. If he caught a youngster trying to sneak a smoke, or misbehaving ever so slightly, the parents knew about it before the kid even got home.

Then, in the early 1960s, a young pharmacist from Bardstown, Robert C. Hurst, took over the "Yellow Corner" and has had it ever since.

There was another frequent visitor to the drugstore in those years—Father James Willett, who never let anyone forget that the Catholic church was always watching. When the young people heard that he was heading in their direction, they fled the drugstore like a flushed covey of quail. If he spotted a young girl wearing shorts or a sleeveless blouse, he sent her home to change. A lot of young couples wouldn't be getting married in the Catholic church if he were around today because their wedding gowns are cut far too low to suit his taste.

Downtown Bardstown was small. There wasn't a lot to do, so the young people had to make their own entertainment. "We had parties on a regular basis as we were growing up," remembers Bobbie Brown. "It was a quiet little community," she adds, "except for Saturdays when everybody kinda came into town to do their weekly shopping." You'd find the kids shooting marbles in at least fifty locations. Those who felt they were a bit too old for marbles could be found at "The Ol' B and B" ice-cream store, where there was a jukebox. Later, you could go to one or both of the two movie theaters downtown.

"By the time you got home, everything you had done on Saturday had already been reported to your parents, so there wasn't any gettin' away with anything much," Bobbie says.

The town is centered on the redbrick courthouse, an imposing fortresslike structure that houses the offices of the circuit clerk, the county sheriff, and several judges, both circuit and district. It's always busy; the courts have a heavy caseload. It's bustling. People are always coming and going. The present courthouse was designed by an architect from Louisville and constructed in 1892 by local craftsmen. To get a better idea of just what this grand old building looks like, if you've ever been to Washington, D.C., and visited the original redbrick Smithsonian, that's the style of architecture used, but the building is on a much, much smaller scale. The style is the same one used for many large government buildings around the country.

The rumble of heavy traffic circles the courthouse in a counterclockwise pattern that was devised by the Romans, only they had monuments and fountains in the center, not buildings.

Third Street, or Main Street as it's most often called, runs north and south from Courthouse Square. Stephen Foster Avenue, known for years as Market Street, runs east and west from the square. The downtown shopping district is small, perhaps seven or eight blocks at most—two blocks north from the courthouse, two blocks to the west, one block to the east, and a few blocks on Flaget Avenue, which crosses Third Street. South from the courthouse and just across the street are residential homes. Talbott Tavern, on the southwest corner of the square, has been there since 1800. Haydon Spalding's clothing store opened its doors in 1854 and has been run by the family ever since. The shops are small and clean. There are people on the sidewalks, inside the stores, buying, and talking, always a favorite pastime. Shopping malls haven't appeared here yet.

If you walk down Third Street, past the drugstore, past Spalding's clothing store for a few minutes, you're in a neighborhood of large, stately homes set well back from the street, their lawns manicured, hedges neatly trimmed. And no fences. The beautiful wrought-iron fences disappeared in World War II scrap drives.

People do a lot of walking here, and you often hear "Hello" and "How are you today?" even if you're a stranger in town.

Although Bardstown is small, there's no shortage of good music, theater, other entertainment, or big-time sports, because Louisville, Lexington, and Nashville, Tennessee, are within easy driving distance.

Going into the 1960s, the whiskey business was still the major industry in these parts. There was a General Electric plant in Louisville, where some of the local people worked. But the distilleries were the major employer, by far. Industrial growth, so far, had been held to a minimum because that's the way the town leaders wanted it. If there was to be growth, they felt, let it be elsewhere.

But if there is one thing here that everyone agrees on, it's patriotism. There's never been a shortage of flags here, or people to wave them. It's the same today as it has been for years. Small flags are stuck in potted plants. Flags hang on front porches. They flutter from flagpoles in front yards. And not just on the Fourth of July.

Over the years, whenever there was a call to arms, Bardstown always answered. Fifty men went off to help Texas fight for independence from Mexico. Only one man returned. Men from Bardstown fought for both the North and the South during the War between the States. They fought in Cuba during the Spanish-American War. They fought and died during World Wars I and II, and again in Korea. The 113th Ordnance Company, the National Guard unit from Bardstown, was activated for duty in the Second World War and also for Korea. It was more or less routine for Bardstown to send its young men off to fight for their country. So Bardstown was no stranger to war, and the pain, the suffering that war brought.

Nevertheless, when the call came, you went, regardless of the consequences, and the entire town stood behind you.

But Vietnam was not like any other war.

It began rather inconspicuously. There were the "advisers,"

professional military men, skilled in the art of war, and trained to pass that knowledge along to the military forces of friendly nations. The first contingent of advisers arrived in Saigon in September of 1950, in the early days of the Korean War, a time when their arrival was hardly noticed. In July 1952, the United States upgraded its diplomatic representation in Saigon from a legation to an embassy. On July 8, 1959, two advisers were killed by hand grenades in a raid by North Vietnamese guerrillas at Bien Hoa. By May 1960, the number of advisers had jumped from 327 to 685. In October 1961, Walt Rostow, a State Department official, and General Maxwell Taylor visited South Vietnam and recommended the introduction of American ground troops to help the South battle the communists from the North. President John F. Kennedy said no to this, but he did increase the number of advisers to 3,200. On the day that President Kennedy was assassinated, November 22, 1963, the number of advisers in South Vietnam had soared to 16,500. There was no turning back now. Several months later, the destroyer *Maddox* reported that it had been attacked by North Vietnamese gunboats in the Gulf of Tonkin. In retaliation, U.S. warplanes bombed North Vietnam for the first time. Then, on August 7, 1964, Congress approved the Tonkin Gulf Resolution, which gave President Lyndon B. Johnson virtual carte blanche to make war in Southeast Asia, which he did. Slowly, almost methodically, it escalated. In a few years, there were more than a half million Americans there. Soon a full-scale war was under way, and it didn't seem to want to go away. It just hung around—forever, it seemed. Eventually, you grew into it, much as you would an old pair of pants handed down from a brother. Washington handed the war down from one age group to another.

"Is this war going to be over before my children are old enough to go?" wondered Dixie Hibbs, the mother of two young sons.

When it finally penetrated Middle America, when it found its way to tiny Bardstown, no one there was prepared for what it would bring. Bardstown would become a symbol of how deep into America the war had reached, and few, if any, communities in this land felt the impact of the war as did the people here.

ONE

The People

The Collins family—Leon, Dorothy, and their three sons—believed in their country, the rewards of hard work, the American dream. Back in the early sixties, they were farming about 350 acres and milking around sixty cows out on Plum Run Road, about six miles from Bardstown, on land that had been in the family for fifty-two years. Wayne, the oldest son, David, and Danny grew up on the farm.

The Collins family was small by Bardstown standards. If a reunion were held, perhaps as many as 140 relatives would show up. The family was well-known and highly regarded by everyone for miles around. Leon ran the farm, it was his life. From morning to night, he worked every day of the year. He was up before dawn, milking and then plowing, planting, cutting hay for the Holsteins. He was tall, about six feet, three inches, and medium weight. His eyes were brown, the same color as his hair had been before it turned gray prematurely. He was very neat, and seldom would you see him in clothing that was soiled, even when busy with farm chores, most of which he did. When he needed help, his sons pitched in, but Wayne and David had full-time jobs elsewhere, and Danny was a youngster.

In the evening, when he watched the news on television and perhaps another program or two, he wore slacks and a dress shirt open at the collar. He was usually in bed by nine o'clock. He wasn't into suits, although he would wear one on special occasions, such as going to church. Every Sunday, the family attended services at Cox's Creek Baptist Church, and would invite their sons' girlfriends to go with them.

But even Sunday was a workday for Leon, because he was up around four A.M. to milk the cows, breakfast with the family, then go to church. After services everyone sat outside in the summer and talked. Then, Dorothy prepared supper. Leon was more like Wayne than David. He was quiet, easygoing. He seemed to take everything in stride. Very seldom did he get excited. No one ever heard him become angry, loud, although he did raise his voice on occasion at the weather, when it hampered his farm work, or when a piece of equipment didn't function properly.

His goal in life was simple: farm his land, make it prosper, then eventually turn it over to one of his sons—probably Danny, because even when he was only eleven or twelve, he seemed to have more interest in the land than did his two older brothers.

Dorothy ran the family. She was tall, too, a few inches under six feet, slender, and very attractive. She, too, had brown eyes and light brown hair that, as had her husband's, grayed prematurely. She kept her hair short on top, a bit longer in the back and along the sides, just enough to cover her ears. Most of the time she wore dresses, nothing bright or flashy, mostly conservative. When she helped out with the farm work, such as carrying milk, she wore slacks, just as she did when she cleaned house. Her home was im-maculate. An excellent seamstress, she made just about all the clothes her sons wore, including their suits. She was a perfectionist. If something was off a sixteenth of an inch, she took it apart and did it again until it was perfect. She also made most of her own clothes, and in later years, she made the maternity clothes for her two daughters-in-law. For Dorothy, sewing was therapy, it was her way of relaxing, and she enjoyed it thoroughly. When she wasn't at the sewing machine, she could be found in the kitchen, where she also excelled. Like her husband, she was calm, easygoing. Once, after she had labored most of an afternoon cleaning her kitchen until it was spotless, Danny brought his dirt-encrusted bicycle in and parked it on the floor she had just scrubbed and waxed. She didn't utter a word. She realized things like this occur when there are children around.

Mrs. Collins loved beautiful, old furniture, and her home was filled with antiques, everywhere but the bedrooms. She had a very old loveseat, a couch, marble-topped chests, a dining room table with eight chairs of walnut, oak, and mahogany. If she didn't like the way one of her antiques looked, she would sand, stain, and refinish it more to her liking. Despite the presence of so many rare pieces of furniture, the Collins home was one in which a person could relax, could feel comfortable. You never felt out of place.

Together, Leon and Dorothy clearly set very high standards for their sons in every walk of life.

It was surprising how many people knew Wayne, because with him, words were miles apart. When you talked about a sphinx, you were talking about Wayne. But when you don't talk a lot, you have a lot of time to listen, and a lot of people appreciate that quality in a person. He was six feet, five inches tall, around 185 pounds, and very good-looking, with brown eyes and dark brown hair. Like his mother and father, he was very neat, and polite with everyone. Although he was quiet, he had a presence. You could feel when he was nearby. When you possess those attributes, you really don't have to say too much. At that, though, he was talking more now than when he was in high school a few years earlier. He didn't like flashy clothes, preferring instead solid colors, subdued, muted. He favored casual shirts and sweaters, but seldom wore jeans. He was living on the farm in the mid-sixties and helped with the chores when help was needed, although he had a full-time job in Louisville with a welding company. Cars have always been important here, and most of the young men had one. If you didn't, you were stuck on the farm, or wherever you happened to live. You couldn't get to a drive-in, you couldn't go to Louisville, you couldn't do a lot of things. Wayne had a 1963 Ford, dark brown and in excellent running condition. He worked on it all the time. He could take it apart and rebuild it, which he often did. Wayne was a cabinetmaker. He had always liked tools and what he could do with them. At first, he used his dad's. When he got older, had a job, some money, he bought his own, and the family garage was full of them. He could, and often did, duplicate antique furniture that was in the family home. He could fix anything—plumbing, repairing, painting. But he stayed away from wiring. He didn't understand electricity and didn't want any part of it.

He and his brother David owned a motorboat and often went waterskiing on nearby Simpson's Lake.

Just about everyone knew David. Those who didn't had probably seen his flashy red convertible around town, or speeding along the back roads. He treated that car as if it were a newborn child. He pampered it, tinkered with it, and it ran perfectly. One never knew when someone might challenge you to a run on the back roads. But neither David nor Wayne was big into drag racing, and their cars weren't really souped up, certainly not like the car owned by their cousin Teddy Collins, which could run with the best of them.

David wasn't a big man, maybe five feet, eight inches, and around 170 pounds. Unlike most of the other young men here, he didn't have much interest in football, basketball, or baseball. His manner of speech was slow, thoughtful. He was warmer than Wayne, and easier to get to know.

David kept the farm machinery in perfect condition. "He could fix anything," his father once said. After he graduated from Bloomfield High School, he went to diesel mechanic school in Nashville, then to work doing what he enjoyed most, working on tractors and other heavy equipment, at Grigsby's, a firm that bought and sold new and used farm implements. He couldn't have been happier.

Danny, the youngest brother, who wouldn't become a teenager until 1968, was clearly following in David's footsteps; you could tell, even when he was eleven, that he had a great interest in motors, engines, all things mechanical. Because of this, Danny was much closer to David than to Wayne. "I will remember him always in the garage, tinkering, fixing things even when he was a youngster," says Mary Collins, Wayne's wife. Danny was fun to be around. He liked to tease, and his mother frequently had to tell him, "Danny, stop picking on Mary." When he got older, Danny, too, worked at

Grigsby's. Even today, if someone has a problem with a tractor, they'll take it to Danny.

Like most young people here at that time, David liked the Beach Boys, country music, Roy Orbison, and Elvis. At some point, say ten years down the road, after he had piled up enough money, he hoped to have a small farm, a few cows, some sheep, grow most of what he needed for the table, and work on big trucks, tractors, and other farm machinery.

That was David on a warm spring day in 1964 as he cruised slowly down Third Street, or Main Street as everyone called it, and noticed a young woman walking toward Courthouse Square, a block away. He couldn't take his eyes off her.

What caught his eye that beautiful day in May was Patricia Aleen Dickerson, eighteen, who had strolled from the office where she worked, Tom Stoner Tax Service. She had just graduated from high school, this was her first full-time job, and it was lunchtime.

Patricia, or Patsy, as she preferred to be called, was quiet, shy, and attractive. When she walked down the street, she did not go unnoticed. She was five feet, six inches tall, and slender. Her light brown hair was in a bouffant coiffure—a little high on top, brushed back on the sides, and maybe a half inch below her ears. Once in a while she would wear a bright ribbon in her hair. She was wearing casual dress slacks that day, a nice blouse, and comfortable shoes that didn't pinch. She seldom wore high heels. Usually, she wore red or light blue. She had one dress, but didn't wear it too often, except to church or a wedding. "If you had one or two dresses back then, well, that was really something," she remembers. Patsy had a good sense of humor and would often joke with friends that "we live so far out, we have to pipe the sunlight in." This wasn't quite true, but when you're young and you don't have a car, a few miles can seem like many.

She wasn't in a hurry as she walked down Main Street. She lived on a farm about three miles from town with her four brothers and five sisters. There were chores in the morning and chores in the evening after she returned from work. Her family had around five hundred acres of hay, corn, soybeans, and tobacco, and about sixty-five dairy cows. So there was plenty of work for everyone. Her mother or father drove her to work in the morning, then picked her up in the evening, so there wasn't much time to socialize with friends. That's why she treasured her few minutes of free time in Bardstown, small as it was, because it gave her the opportunity to be with friends from high school, to chitchat with others she had grown up with. She knew just about everyone in town. In fact, it would be unusual for her to see someone she didn't know.

Patsy was on her way to Walgreen's drugstore for her usual lunch, a Coke and two small packages of cheese crackers. The drugstore was one block from her office on Main Street, right on Courthouse Square and a few feet from the old post office.

If you sat at the lunch counter long enough, eventually you would see every young person in town. That was their hangout, their midday gathering place. They were there more to talk than to eat, to pick up the latest gossip, to find out who was dating whom. "I could meet people my age at the drugstore," she remembers, "and that was fun." And if you missed seeing someone at Walgreen's, you could probably see that person in the evening at the Dairy Chef, across from My Old Kentucky Home, where they all went to have a Coke, hamburger, or French fries. Mostly to talk.

At first, Patsy didn't notice the bright red convertible with the top down, cruising slowly down Main Street, around the courthouse, and back up the other side. But each time the car passed her, it slowed to a crawl. By this time, she knew the driver was checking her out, so "I kinda slowed down a little bit, you know, keeping my eye on him to the point that you don't want him to know you're watching.

"That's all I saw on the whole block at that time, just him," Patsy remembers, "and I was thinking, 'Man, I'd like to meet him,' 'cause he was really good-looking."

At first, he didn't wave. Nevertheless, Patsy wondered who he was. "He must have slipped through a crack," she thought, "because I thought I knew everyone around here."

Next day, same time, same routine. Patsy was on her way to lunch. The red convertible with the beautiful white top was there, cruising slowly, but not stopping each time it passed her. Only this time, the driver waved, sort of. He lifted one hand above the door, then bent the fingers a few inches. "He waved," Patsy recalls, "but it was kinda weak.

"So I waved back, but just a little," she says.

That night, she called a few friends, described the car and the driver, and asked if they knew who he was.

"A bright red convertible with a spotless white top? That has to be David Collins," one friend told her.

"He went to Bloomfield High School," another added.

"He lives on a farm about six miles from town," a third friend said. When all the reports were in, she had a very positive picture of this young fellow who had a great smile, who had caught her fancy. So she decided she would meet him.

Next day, he was out there again, cruising, waiting for her to go to lunch. "This time, he really waved," Patsy remembers. "So I waved back."

Then they made eye contact.

"He pulled over, stopped, smiled that great big ear-to-ear smile, and asked me if I'd like to go get something to eat."

"Yes," she said, and got into the car.

"We were both too excited to eat, so we drove around until the last minute of our lunch break, then he took me back to work," she remembers. "Anyway, I was too bashful to eat in front of him. It was two or three months before I'd even drink a Coke with him. I was afraid I'd do something wrong.

"I was really shy," she adds.

"All I could do was think of him while we were riding around that day," she remembers. "Having lunch never entered my mind.

"While I was in the car with him, I kept telling myself things like, 'Don't get excited.' 'Don't do anything silly.' 'Just calm down.'

"I don't remember if I got excited, did anything silly, or ever calmed down." But she does remember that "he had on his work clothes when we met, and I'll never forget how neat and clean he was.

"After he dropped me off at work that day, I remember telling myself that he wouldn't give me a second look, that he'd forget me."

But he didn't. That night, after she returned home from work, the telephone rang in the early evening. It was David.

"I liked him immediately," Patsy remembers. "That day that we met, well, that was my lucky day."

For Patsy Dickerson and David Collins, it was classic young love. Boy meets girl, they fall in love, get married and live happily . . .

———

Mary Nalley and a few of her friends were at the Dairy Chef one summer day having a Coke and, as usual, talking, when a very nice-looking fellow in a Ford drove in. "Some of the girls knew him, but I had not seen him before," she remembers. "He had a real nice car," she adds. "The top was down, and it was a nice dark brown."

"I'd sure like a ride in that convertible," one of the girls remarked.

"Sure. Hop in," Wayne responded.

The girls all climbed in. Mary sat up front, next to the driver. She remembers how polite he was, how he didn't try to impress them.

"We talked a little, but he was shy, I was shy, so mostly we just rode around," Mary said.

"He had just broken up with a girlfriend, and I had just broken up with a guy I was engaged to, so we were both kinda leery of each other," Mary explains.

Despite this, they hit it off, and they started going out once a week, on a Friday or a Saturday. Soon it was Friday and Saturday.

Mary was five feet nine, slender, with reddish-brown hair. She wasn't as conservative as Wayne in her dress: she liked bright colors in her blouses, sweaters, and skirts. She was a sharp dresser and worked in a clothing store, the Lincoln Shop, a few doors from the town square. She could sell clothes and soon worked herself into a position where she was able to assist in the buying. After work, the young people would meet at the Dairy Chef simply because the parking lot there was bigger than the one at any other drive-in. More cars could pull in, more people would be there, you could mingle more. The thing she liked best about Wayne Collins was his sense of humor. He could laugh at himself.

"One time, we were eating at a drive-in in Louisville, and I was fooling around with a small package of catsup," Mary says. "I don't know what I did, but it just seemed to explode. The catsup shot out and hit him on the neck and ran down his throat onto his shirt. All I could do was sit there and laugh. And he laughed about it, too.

"I guess that's why I liked him," Mary remarks. "I knew three weeks after we met that he was the one that I wanted to spend the rest of my life with." They were a matched pair. One complementing the other.

They were together for about five months; then one fall day, he matter-of-factly said, "I kinda wish Christmas would hurry up and get here."

"Why?"

"Well, I was thinking of giving you a ring."

"That was just his way of proposing," Mary explains, "but I already knew what was on his mind. He just had to say it in his own way."

━━━━━

Ronald Earl Simpson and Deanna Durbin met the way most young people meet in these parts—riding around in cars. A car full of girls, another full of guys. Someone waves, hollers. Someone in the other car responds with a wave of the hand or a shout. That's how Ronnie and Deanna became acquainted.

"Actually, I don't remember seeing him," she says, "but I guess he kind of singled me out. He was a big football player in Bardstown, and he was loud, outgoing, and confident."

Ronnie was five feet, nine inches, solid, muscular, with the build of an athlete, which he was. He could play just about any sport. Deanna liked that because she was athletic herself, and often played softball, volleyball, and badminton at Bernheim Park, where young couples frequently went on weekends.

Deanna liked his hazel eyes, the way he dressed—jeans, bright, colorful shirts, usually with a lot of brown, which was his favorite color. When he was in high school, he worked part-time at a service station. After graduation, he worked briefly at the General Electric plant in Louisville, then became a lineman with the Salt River Rural Electric Cooperative. He liked that type of work, outdoors, rugged. He was good with his hands, liked to build things, enjoyed carpentry. His family owned rental homes in the area, and Ronnie worked on them, fixing a roof that leaked, replacing a door or a window. He was always busy.

Deanna, after graduation from high school, went to work for a law firm in Bardstown.

She liked to wear her brown hair high on top, teased. Her dresses and skirts stopped just above the knee. She favored slacks, shorts, outdoor clothes. She was five feet, four inches, and just a few pounds over a hundred. Rock and roll, the Beach Boys, and a little bit of Elvis, picnics in the forest, parties, and dancing were at the top of her "like" list.

Very determined and independent, she often set goals for herself, and reached most of them. "I liked to prove to myself that I could do things," she remembers. "I knew back then I could make it on my own, if I ever had to."

"Deanna wasn't the kind of person who would talk endlessly and say nothing," a close friend says. "When she talked, she had something to say."

Bardstown was small and surrounded by farmland. Although Ronnie and Deanna lived in town, their lives weren't markedly different from the lives of those who lived on farms. They'd all get together evenings and on weekends at Dairy Chef or in the park, or would drive to Louisville together. Farm life was closely tied with life in the town. Patsy, who lived on a farm, and Deanna were close friends.

When Deanna and Ronnie started dating, Ronnie owned a blue-and-white 1955 Chevy, which he washed and waxed every Sunday morning. Then they would cruise around town, maybe go to a drive-in. He liked to race it on the back roads, too, just like all the other young guys. Sometimes they would sneak onto the Bluegrass Parkway, which was nearly finished, but not yet open to the public, and race until the police showed up.

Mostly, though, he liked to race in sanctioned events in nearby Campbellsville, where he won several trophies.

They weren't a twosome yet, but they did go out a lot together. One night, though, when he was supposed to call and didn't, she went out with someone else.

"When Ronnie found out about it, he quickly gave me his class ring, which meant that we were going steady," Deanna remembers.

There were occasional ups and downs, but they always went back together. A couple of years passed, they were still together, so, quite naturally, their thoughts turned to the future, to marriage, a family.

███████

About this time, 1964 and into 1965, the fighting in Vietnam was escalating at a rapid pace as America fought history's first television war. People around the country were beginning to hear such grim words as "body bag" and "body count" on the nightly news. They were seeing, too, in their living rooms, the brutal beating, torture, and killing of prisoners of war. There were growing antiwar protests on the campuses and then in the streets. But the impact of the fighting in faraway Vietnam had not yet penetrated small-town America, and had hardly caused a ripple in Bardstown. The people here, by and large, were doing what they had always done when their country went to war—they were standing behind their government, solidly and proudly. They figured that their leaders in Washington had the best information available and would thus make the proper decisions. So they backed them and their decisions.

In these early days of Vietnam, the *Kentucky Standard*, the weekly newspaper here, supported the war.

"I think we supported the idea because we felt like it was the thing to do," remembers Elizabeth Spalding, longtime editor of the paper, who is now retired. "After all, you have a national administration that has a lot more information than you have, so, more or less, you put your faith in your leaders." This wasn't an unusual feeling, around this time, since seventy-six percent of people around the country placed their faith in their leaders, trusting the government to do the right thing, most of the time.

"The older people seemed to favor the war at that time," Spalding says, "and the younger people weren't too interested in going."

"At first, I thought it was one of the things we got to do, and let's get on with it," says former Mayor Gus Wilson, a veteran of the Second World War.

Most young people here were more interested in things like dating, graduating from high school, finding a job, perhaps even moving away if no work was to be found. Vietnam was not on their minds. It was a time, instead, when they were in the early stages of selecting a partner for life, when relationships were developing into commitments that they hoped would last a lifetime, through the good and the bad.

This was a quality group of young people, mostly in their late teens and early twenties. There would be sadness for some, happiness for others. In the years ahead, the community's civic and elected leaders would emerge from this group.

Ronnie and Libby Hibbs first saw each other when she was fifteen and he was twenty-one. "He ran around with my older brother at the time," she remembers. Soon Ronnie began calling her, then started dropping around the family farm, way out on Solitude Road. They started seeing each other at a nearby roller-skating rink. Both were excellent skaters. "Daddy had a barn with a concrete floor, and I used to skate there," she recalls. "I remember how excited I was when I got my first pair of skates, because back then, you didn't get but one thing for Christmas.

"Ronnie had a pretty car, a 1962 Ford Galaxie, that he had fixed up," she remembers. "It was baby blue. I used to see him in it, and I did like that car." It was fast, too, perhaps the fastest around town, and seldom did anyone catch it.

Ronnie was five feet, eight inches and of slight build, maybe 140 pounds. His eyes were blue, the color of his car; he liked jeans and long-sleeved shirts, which were always rolled up to the elbow. If one thing stood out about him, it had to be his smile. That's why everyone referred to him as "Smiley."

Libby was five foot seven, trim, slim, with green eyes and blond hair that fell to her shoulders. Skirts and dresses stopped at the knees. She liked knit slacks and colorful blouses with a lot of red. They both liked music of the fifties and sixties—the Supremes, Elvis, the Beach Boys. The two radio stations in the area played the music they liked back then and are still playing it today, and they're still listening.

Libby was the H-O-R-S-E champion of Solitude Road. She could shoot the eye out of the basket—in this case, an old bicycle rim with the spokes removed that was nailed to the barn. She beat all comers—boys, girls, guys, gals, including a brother who played on the high school team.

Libby liked Ronnie the first time he ever asked her out. She was too young to date alone, her parents felt, but they did let her double-date with her cousin and her boyfriend because the cousin was a few years older.

"We really got serious in 1966," she says, "and when that happened, my parents tried to keep us apart. They really wanted me to go to college. They even paid my tuition and bought all my clothes.

"Once Ronnie found out that I was planning on going to college, well, we talked it over, and we decided to run off and get married, which we did."

At first, they couldn't find anyone to marry them because she was only seventeen, but they kept trying. Then they reached Jamestown, Tennessee, found a justice of the peace, P. G. Crooks, who agreed to do the ceremony, and they were married in a furniture store.

"My family wanted to kill me and him both when they found out, but about three weeks later, once they calmed down, they loved him," Libby says.

"But they were very, very upset at first," she adds, with just a little trace of laughter.

They stayed with an aunt, Lottie Hibbs, for a few weeks, and then bought a house trailer and lived in nearby High Grove, which had one store and, on its best day, perhaps as many as fifty people. Here, Ronnie had a small auto body shop, some paint, tools, a sander, and he was always pounding out a dent in a fender, repainting it.

━━━━━━━

By this time, 1966, Raymond S. Ford had been in the army for about two and a half years, something that his mother had always wanted him to do. She felt that it would be good for him, that it would give her son the opportunity to see some of the world, because there wasn't enough money at home to get him more than a few miles from Bardstown. He came from a large family—four brothers and seven sisters.

Since he didn't care for high school and wasn't interested in going to college, his mother, Bertha Ford, was afraid that he'd just hang around town and not amount to much of anything. So she encouraged him to enlist and let the government pay for his travels. Raymond graduated from high school in June of 1963. The following month, he joined the army. He had no problem with discipline. In fact, he thrived on situations that required discipline, and he liked to be around those who were older. So the army suited him just fine.

"Mother didn't like the idea of the boys' just staying around here and not amounting to anything," explains Brenda, one of his sisters. "So she always kind of pushed the military as a way out, as a way of seeing the world." Two of his brothers are in the army; one of them served in Saudi Arabia. A third brother is in the navy, and the fourth works and lives in Bardstown.

Raymond was home for two weeks in December of 1965. On December 14, he left to rejoin his unit, Company D, Second Battalion, Twelfth Cavalry Regiment, to prepare for shipment to Vietnam.

"I remember when my brother left," Brenda says softly, as if it had just happened. "I was going to school. He told me I'd see him later. 'This time next year I'll be here,' he said."

Bertha Ford received a letter from her son on February 19, 1966, in which he told her that he was fine and that his company was preparing to go into battle.

The next day, February 20, Raymond Ford was dead. He was twenty-one.

Police officer Adrian O'Daniel knew everyone in town back then, especially the young people, for certain the dragsters. He was on a first-name basis with every one of them. He knew their cars on sight and would follow them if he thought one was heading for a back road. Crime wasn't a big headache back in the early sixties. Nor were drugs. "The biggest problem we had back then was drag racing," O'Daniel recalls. "They were always out there."

O'Daniel, who has since retired from the Bardstown police department as a captain, was always out there, too, and when the young people saw him approaching, they scattered. Even so, they respected him. He could talk to them, he could talk with them, regardless of the color of their skin. They were on the same wavelength. No one ever gave him a hard time.

O'Daniel knew the Ford family well, and remembers that day, February 20, 1966, as if it were yesterday.

The rain was coming down about as hard as he had ever seen. And it was cold. Very cold. He wondered when it would turn to snow. Or, worse, whether it would turn to ice. That would make the rest of his shift a nightmare, for sure. On second thought, it couldn't possibly be worse than what he had to do now.

Very carefully he guided his patrol car out Stephen Foster Highway, hoping that the oncoming traffic was as conscious of the terrible driving conditions as he was. He slowed to a crawl, then swung left across the oncoming lane and pulled up as close as he could to the front entrance to Jones' Kentucky Home Restaurant. It seemed to be raining even harder as he got out of his car and walked slowly toward the steps. He really wasn't eager to go inside. Nevertheless, he opened the door and walked in and spotted Bertha Ford in the kitchen area, and moved in that direction. He had known Mrs. Ford and her children for years.

He spoke to Mrs. Ford for a few moments, quietly, respectfully, somberly. "Bertha, your son Raymond has been killed in Vietnam. . . ." She was stunned, shaken, speechless, as only a mother could be at a moment like this. He placed an arm around her shoulders to steady her. Then she sat down. Nothing was said for several minutes. "I'll get your coat, Bertha, then I'll take you home."

Wanda, one of Bertha's daughters, was at home that Sunday afternoon and saw the police car stop out front. She saw O'Daniel walk around to the other side, help her mother out, then up to the front door. Once inside, Bertha collapsed into a chair, stunned, in a state of shock.

Then O'Daniel told Wanda and several other members of the family: "Your brother Raymond has been killed in Vietnam."

They sat in silence, in disbelief, for a long time. The only movement in the room was that of tears streaming down their cheeks.

Brenda, who was thirteen at that time, had been out with friends that day. "I remember coming into the house. Everyone was there, sitting and crying," Brenda says. "I asked what happened, and everybody just looked at me. They didn't say anything." Then someone told her. "I was just stunned. It was like I really didn't hear what they said."

Later that day, Mrs. Ford received a telegram from the army confirming that her son had been killed. The telegrams were all pretty much the same. Only the names were different. A few words expressing the government's sorrow. A few more words concerning the cause of death. Before this was over, more than fifty-eight thousand telegrams would be sent to families around the country. They were worded pretty much like this:

WESTERN UNION
TELEGRAM

FEB 20 66   WASHINGTON, DC

BERTHA FORD   DONT PHONE DONT DLVR

BARDSTOWN KY   BTWN 10PM AND 6AM

THE SECRETARY OF THE ARMY HAS ASKED ME TO EXPRESS HIS DEEP REGRET THAT YOUR SON, SPE-CIALIST FOUR RAYMOND S. FORD, DIED IN VIET-NAM ON 20 FEB 1966 AS A RESULT OF WOUND RECEIVED WHILE ON COMBAT OPERATIONS WHEN HIT BY FRAGMENT FROM ENEMY GRE-

NADE. PLEASE ACCEPT MY DEEPEST SYMPATHY.
THIS CONFIRMS PERSONAL NOTIFICATION MADE
BY A REPRESENTATIVE OF THE SECRETARY OF
THE ARMY.

> KENNETH G. WICKHAM,
> MAJOR GENERAL, USA,
> THE ADJUTANT GENERAL

Early Monday morning, a khaki-color sedan from close-by Fort Knox stopped in front of the Ford home. An army chaplain got out, walked up to the front door, knocked. The family was there, waiting. He talked with Mrs. Ford, and helped with the funeral arrangements. Army SP/4 Raymond S. Ford was laid to rest a week later, the first of Bardstown's young men to die in Vietnam. There would be others.

Remembering the death of Ford, Elizabeth Spalding remarks, "I think you feel like, did he give his life for a true cause?"

The death of young Ford was the lead story on page one of the *Kentucky Standard*. There was a four-column headline above the story and a one-column photograph of the black soldier. You couldn't help noticing that Vietnam was beginning to reach out and touch Middle America. As for Bertha Ford, she remembers, "I was never for the war, and so far as the older people that I knew, well, they hated it."

At this particular time, 1965 and into 1966, it really didn't matter here whether you supported the war, opposed it, or were indifferent. The war was not that big an issue here. What you did was simple. You supported the fighting men who were there, you supported their families, their loved ones here at home, and above all, you stood behind those who had been to Vietnam and had returned. You did not taunt them, you did not ridicule them. There was no question about this.

To stress this support for those in the military, Sunday, July 31, 1966, was set aside as "Vietnam Day" in Bardstown. The mayor, Gus Wilson, and the chamber of commerce held a reception, open to the public, in Bardstown High School, to honor Vietnam veterans, their families, and families of men serving in Vietnam. Col. Hal G. Moore, a West Point graduate and much-decorated veteran of Vietnam, was honored while home on leave. So was Bertha Ford. Special invitations went out to wives or parents of thirty-five other servicemen, only slightly different from the one below that went to Mrs. Ford.

July 26, 1966

Mrs. Bertha Ford
West Brasher Avenue
Bardstown, Kentucky

Dear Mrs. Ford:

The City of Bardstown and the Chamber of Commerce is holding a reception to honor all Viet Nam veterans and their families on Sunday, July 31, 1966 at Bardstown High School from 1:00 to 3:00 P.M. This is to honor any men who have served or are serving in Viet Nam.

We would consider it a distinct pleasure if you could be present at this reception with your immediate family. There will be a receiving committee at the door to have a special name tag for you.

Col. Hal Moore, who has recently returned from Viet Nam will also be one of our distinguished guests and has expressed a personal desire to meet you.

This will be open to the public and you are encouraged to ask any of your friends or family.

Very truly yours,
Guthrie M. Wilson
Mayor

GMW:ls

There were no speeches, no special tribute to anyone, certainly not to Colonel Moore, who preferred to remain in the background.

"This was a happy occasion then, because in 1966, there

was a kind of feeling we were winning, you know," the mayor explains.

All things considered, it was a good day for the crowd of a thousand or more that showed up, something that many of them needed, because they were beginning to envision their children, other young people in the community, approaching draft age, growing into the war, if it didn't go away.

Some of those honored that day were Mrs. Malcolm Geoghegan and children, Mrs. Betty Stephens, Mr. and Mrs. Harold Searcy, Mrs. Lois Ballard, Mrs. George Fraim, Mrs. Edwin Smith, and Mr. and Mrs. Robert Taylor, whose three sons, all Marines, would serve in Vietnam. George Kenneth Taylor was wounded in February 1966, and was back in action. He was a staff sergeant. Sgt. Paul Edwin Taylor had already completed one tour and was on a second, and Cpl. William Russell Taylor was on his way to Vietnam. This was a Marine family, body and soul.

"It was very hard when George joined," says Frances Taylor, mother of the three Marines, "but we raised them to be independent, and this is what he wanted to do more than anything else—join the Marines."

Paul Edwin Taylor joined next.

Finally, William Russell Taylor signed up.

"He [William] had his heart set on joining the corps from the moment George came home from boot camp," his mother explains.

"In the early years of the war, when our government was sending them all over there, well, we were U.S.A., all the way, so we supported this," she says.

"I remember the ceremony at the high school," she adds. "It was a show of our patriotism, as usual. Remember, we've been doing this since the Revolutionary War.

"And I remember when George was wounded. I was sad, and very apprehensive, but I never changed my point of view," Mrs. Taylor continues.

"In those early years, I don't think any of us here understood anything about the Vietnamese people, the war, or that part of the world."

Mrs. Taylor's youngest son, William, had been home on leave

in May of 1966. He left June 1 to return to his unit and at that time said he thought he'd be going to Vietnam.

"I received a letter from him on the first of July saying he was all right," Frances Taylor says. "That was the last letter I received from him."

William Russell Taylor's wife, Barbara, was living at that time with her parents, Mr. and Mrs. Bill Downs, in Bardstown. The Taylors were at their home in close-by New Haven when their telephone rang on August 28.

"Can you come over to the Downses' house?" It was a priest from St. Joseph's Cathedral calling. He was with Barbara and her parents, along with two officers from Fort Knox.

"Are you alone?" the priest asked.

"No, my husband is here," she answered.

"Would you both come over to the Downses' home? I have bad news. Your son has been killed in Vietnam."

"I had three sons there at that time, but since he was calling from Barbara's home, I knew it was Russell. I was stunned. I was speechless. I couldn't move for a while," Frances Taylor remembers.

When she arrived at Barbara's, one of the officers told her that her son, who had been in Vietnam only four days, had been caught in an ambush and died of his wounds, the second fatality from the area. He was twenty years old.

"After that, I think we began to question the war a little more," his mother says. "I think we were beginning to feel like, 'Well, let's get it over with, or let's get out of there.'"

━━━━━

The year 1968 was a bad one for the war effort, the country, and Bardstown. The United States had been heavily committed in Vietnam for three years now, and we had not ground down the enemy. Most of the time we couldn't find them. The generals optimistically saw success ahead, despite one failure after another. At this point, the war could best be described as a series of blunders. Then the Tet offensive of January took the fighting out of the jungle and into the hamlets, villages, big cities, to the doorstep of Gen. William

C. Westmoreland, the American commander, and to the grounds of the American embassy. Tet began with about eighty-four thousand enemy troops on the attack. When it was over, an estimated forty-eight thousand were dead, wounded, or captured, according to our figures. If these figures were accurate, this could be described as a great victory for the United States. Nevertheless, Tet did not sit well with the people at home, where the government was slowly but steadily losing the war, politically and psychologically. Demonstrations against the war on the campuses across the country were growing in size and violence. There weren't enough police to control the antiwar protests in the cities.

In Washington, there was a very secret, very small group of high-level officials in the White House and the Defense Department working toward deescalation and trying to convince President Johnson that a reduction in troop strength would eventually lead to peace talks.

Deescalation or peace talks, it didn't matter which for the family of army Pvt. William David Price, who was killed on March 18 of that year, the third young man from the Bardstown area to die in Vietnam. The war now was starting to take a heavy toll on Bardstown and beginning to drain the regular armed forces of its fighting men. The generals began to clamor for more bodies, perhaps as many as two hundred thousand. Solid leadership and a firm commitment seemed to be lacking in the highest levels of the military and the government.

Then, on Sunday, March 31, the president stunned the nation with his totally unexpected disclosure that he would not seek reelection. At the same time, Johnson said that there would be a deescalation in the fighting and a partial halt in the bombing, in an effort to spur peace talks with North Vietnam.

But on April 11, Defense Secretary Clark Clifford announced a call-up of the reserves and the National Guard totaling 24,500 men, with 10,000 slated for duty in Vietnam. Included were 570 guardsmen from Kentucky, most of them with the Second Battalion, 138th Artillery. Clifford hinted that more might be mobilized in the future.

TWO

The Call-Up

Secretary of Defense Clark Clifford's summoning of the National Guard to federal service sent shock waves throughout the state of Kentucky. It hit Bardstown like a bolt of lightning. No one expected it. Many, in fact, looked upon the Guard as a means to avoid winding up in Vietnam. Living in Bardstown in those turbulent years was much like living in the eye of a hurricane. The war swirled around you, lingering just long enough to hurt a few people, before moving on. No one had ever burned a draft card in Bardstown. There were no antiwar protests in the streets. Nor did anyone of draft age run off to Canada. But not too many people were eager to go to Vietnam, either, and life, after the call-up on April 11, 1968, did not go on as usual. Nor would Bardstown ever be the same.

"I heard about the call-up while I was at lunch," remembers Deanna Durbin, whose marriage to Ronnie Simpson was but a few months away.

"I was scared, and when I got back to work, I wanted to break out in tears, but I didn't," she says. "I wanted to go see him because I was very upset." She saw him after work, around four-thirty, at his mother's house, where he lived.

"He was in the kitchen, and I remember looking at him.

He looked at me, and I wanted to cry." But again she held back the tears.

"He came over, took my hand, and we went outside and over to the house next door that he had just bought for us, and we decided right then that we'd rent it, for now." Then she broke down, and the tears flowed down her cheeks.

The next night, they went out on a date and discussed the call-up, how it would affect their future, their lives, their wedding plans. "But he was upset," she says, "and felt that he should be with the guys in the battery, but he called me about nine and we talked until eleven-thirty."

Patsy Dickerson and David Collins had been going together for about four years now, and she was as happy as she had ever been. Things were going so well, in fact, they planned to marry on May 23, just a few weeks away. "I had been around some guys, they had come out to the farm to play basketball, and I had dated a few, but I'd never been around anyone like David," she reminisces.

"We set the wedding date a full year in advance so we wouldn't have to rush around at the last minute making plans, changing plans," she remembers. "We wanted everything well planned and well organized so that when the day came, all we had to do was walk into the church.

"But I guess somebody bigger than life said, 'No, Patsy, that isn't to be.'"

Patsy was at home the day she found out David's unit had been activated. "I didn't like it one bit," she says. "But David always said if he had to go, he had to go. But I still didn't like it one bit.

"David never expected that he'd be called up," she says. "I don't think many of them expected they'd be called up.

"David was surprised, and his parents were totally shocked, because not only did David have to go, his brother Wayne went also," Patsy continues. "And my mother was really upset, too."

For David and Patsy, the call-up couldn't have come at a worse time. He was doing some bulldozing work and had three jobs to finish before he left. He was also helping his father put up hay on the farm. And they had just purchased a house, which he was fixing up so they could move in after their wedding.

"After the call-up, we wound up changing the date to May third at the last minute so that we could get married before David went on active duty," she recalls. "It was chaos, let me tell you.

"But there was no question that we would delay the wedding until after he came back," she says. "That was absolutely out of the question. In fact, we didn't even discuss it."

Patsy's family always said she'd have a dozen kids.

"We certainly planned on having a family and living on a farm, with animals and tractors, things like that," she adds. "We both loved that kind of life. And kids."

"I was stunned," recalls Betty McClure, wife of Tom McClure, commanding officer of the local Guard unit, Battery C. "Everyone in town was stunned. I heard about it on the radio. I had not expected anything of this sort, and I was shocked.

"I knew that it would change our lives," she remembers.

Kenneth (Buck) Harned heard about the call-up in a rather unusual way. An electrician, he was installing a television in a motel room and had just turned it on to see if it worked. He was fine-tuning it when he heard: ". . . five units of the Kentucky National Guard have been activated . . ."

"Well, I'll be damned," he remembers muttering to himself.

Harned was one of the oldest men in the unit. In fact, his time was up when he got word of the call-up, so he reenlisted just so he could remain with the guys.

"My wife thought I was crazy," he says, "but she didn't try to stop me.

"I just decided I'd go and I figured on coming back, maybe not in the same condition I left."

Thomas R. Ice, a second lieutenant and the fire direction officer for the battery at that time, was on his way to the National Guard armory at the fairgrounds in Louisville when he heard of the call-up on the radio.

"I remember that I was shocked," he says. "That's the best way of putting it. I had no idea at all that this would happen." At that time, Capt. Harold Loy was in command at the armory.

"When I got there, he was already there, along with his staff, fielding questions," Ice says. "The phones were beginning to ring. Two or three of the men had already come by to find out what was happening, what this meant.

"But we didn't know, we really didn't have much news of anything for several days," continues Ice, who joined the Guard in 1964 because he could see the draft looming in his future.

———

Joy Brooks, a young college student, was sitting in the kitchen when she heard the horrible news on the radio. "It was a complete and total shock," she remembers. "I was stunned. I kept wanting to hear more, to make sure that I hadn't gotten something wrong." She ran into the living room, flipped on the television, and "the bad news was all over the place."

Her boyfriend, Jerry Janes, was sitting at the lunch counter in a small restaurant close to the distillery where he worked. Usually, there were several others with him. Today, he was alone, eating, watching television, when the scheduled program was interrupted with a news bulletin: "Kentucky National Guard, Battery C, 138th, called to active duty . . ." He was speechless at first, then he turned to the person on the next stool and asked:

"Did he say . . . ?"

"That's exactly what he said. Do you belong to that unit?"

"I sure as hell do."

"I was very surprised. I was shocked," Janes remembers. "I couldn't believe it. I just couldn't believe it." He quickly paid his bill and rushed back to work. "Some of the guys there had heard it on the radio," Janes says, "and when they saw me, they said, 'Damn, Jerry, you got called up.'" He left work early that afternoon and rushed to the armory. He saw the first sergeant, Pat Simpson, and asked, "Is that right, Pat?"

"That's right, Jerry." Jodie Haydon was there. Kent Bischoff came in a short time later. Then others trickled in as they got off work. It was depressing. They talked for a while. A few others came in, all wanting more information.

"Is it true?" one asked.

"When do we leave? Where do we go?" another wondered. Then the telephone in Simpson's office began to ring. And ring. And ring. It continued ringing until everyone had left.

Janes left and drove to Joy's house. She heard the knock on the back door and dashed back into the kitchen, and saw Jerry standing there.

"Have you heard the news?" he asked breathlessly.

"It can't be true, it can't be," she said, visibly disturbed.

They were both eager for more news, to confirm some of the rumors that had already begun circulating. So they sat in front of the television, hanging on every word. "We talked for a long time and came to the conclusion that if we'd take care of each other, together we'll come through this."

Then they heard the phone. "Friends and relatives of mine, and Jerry's, wanted to know if we had heard the news, if it were true." Word of the call-up spread through the town like a grass fire in a windstorm. In a few hours, it was all over Nelson County. "People would stop you on the street to see if you knew something they didn't," Joy says. "They'd shout from one car to another. If you were on the sidewalk, they'd slow down to talk." But details were sketchy, solid information lacking.

At the time of the call-up, Joy was a sophomore. She and Jerry had planned to get married between her junior and senior years, but later decided to postpone it until after her graduation. Jerry, who had been in college, decided that he didn't want to continue, which virtually ensured his being drafted. "Someone who knew Jerry and was on the draft board told him he would soon be drafted," Joy said. He didn't want to go into the regular army. He thought about the air force, but that was a four-year hitch. "In all honesty, I joined the Guard to beat the draft," Janes explains. "I thought I could serve six months, and then be home, a weekend warrior situation, and then get out after a two-year hitch, and possibly stay out of Vietnam.

"To be honest, I did not think I'd ever be in Vietnam. I just didn't think the National Guard would be called up," he continues. So he signed up in 1967.

"Jerry and I were in high school when the war in Vietnam began, and we talked about it," Joy says. "We talked more about it as the war continued and Jerry got older. We knew that it was in his, in our, future, and we were concerned. If you were a boy, you knew you had to go, or get in college. The gamble was whether the war would be over by the time you got out.

"It was on my mind," she recalls. "When I was a freshman in college, I wrote three term papers, one on the Vietnam war, another on the legality of the draft, and I forget what the third one was. So you can see that Vietnam was on my mind. Those essays, by the way, didn't cause a ripple.

"With Jerry in the Guard in 1968, I was feeling very relaxed. I felt sure that he was not going to be called up. I felt sure he wasn't going to have to go. The Guard is only called up in time of national emergency," she notes, "and this was not a national emergency.

"We felt good about this, we felt patriotic," Joy continues. "We felt Jerry was doing the right thing, that he was serving his country, but wouldn't have to get into that political mess called Vietnam.

"Opposition to the war in this area very definitely came from the campuses," she adds, "but it didn't go into the streets, like it did in so many other cities."

After completing his basic training, Jerry was sent to Arizona for advanced instruction. While there, he met an old master sergeant who had two hitches in Vietnam under his belt. "You will end up in Vietnam before this is all said and done," the sergeant told Janes. "I laughed and told him, 'No way. I don't think so,'" Janes remembers. "I told him he was crazy. But that stuck with me, and I remembered it afterwards—after we got called up, I thought about that a whole lot. Turns out he was a lot smarter than me."

By evening, the town was in turmoil. Guardsmen, wives, girlfriends, parents—everyone was frantically searching out bits of information, but finding none. They wanted to know when the men would be leaving. Where they would be going.

Pat Simpson, at the age of twenty-eight, perhaps the youngest first sergeant in the army, heard about the call-up from his wife. "She heard about it on television and called me," he says. At first, he didn't believe it. " 'Well,' I said, 'it must be something else.' So I turned the radio on, and I heard it then. That was about five minutes to twelve.

"I remember watching 'Meet the Press' one Sunday about six months prior to this. They were interviewing a couple of senators or congressmen, and they said that it was just a matter of time before there was a partial call-up of the Guard and the reserves," Simpson says.

"I never really thought much about it," he adds. "It did surprise me when they did call us. But I never thought that much about it, really."

Then the telephone began to ring, and the guys started coming in.

"Well, what about it?" they asked Simpson. "It's true," he said.

"They were all excited about it," he remembers, "but not initially concerned. Later on, once it sunk in, they became concerned.

"At first, it was sort of disbelief," he says.

███████

Tom McClure joined the Guard in 1962 at the age of twenty-two as a private E-2, the lowest rank in the army. It was that, or face the draft, which was looking more likely. But he had two years of reserve officer training in college, so he was sent away to receive instruction in how to become an officer and a gentleman.

"The first time I ever heard anything about Vietnam was at the Fort Sill, Oklahoma, artillery school, where I was in the officer candidate school," he says. "I learned there that we had advisers in Vietnam, but I really didn't know what they were, or did." He was commissioned a second lieutenant in 1964, and took over command of Battery C six weeks before it was called to active duty.

"I don't guess I really thought about being called up," he says. "There was always the possibility, but I didn't really think about it."

Although he was the battery commander, he was one of the last in the unit to hear the bad news. "Pat Simpson, the only full-time person in the unit, called my wife to see if I had heard the news," he explains.

"Heard what?" Betty McClure asked Simpson, who managed the armory, who watched the store.

"He's been called up," Simpson told her.

Most of the men in the unit knew about it by midafternoon, but McClure didn't find out until he got home from work that afternoon, and his wife told him, "I think you've been called to active duty."

"When Tom came home that night, we talked about it," she says, although he didn't have much information. "He told me he had thirty days to get things in order before he left for Fort Hood, Texas." That meant they had a month to reorganize their lives, to resolve important matters such as handling money. She would now be paying the bills. Drawing up a will. Filling out the myriad government forms that the military requires of dependents. Making arrangements for their son's schooling. Michael was about six, and in four months, he would begin his first year in class. They also had a daughter, Charlotte, who was two. "My life was continually chasing after them," she says.

"They didn't talk too much about the war at that time," McClure remembers, "and it wasn't a burning issue until you heard you were going. Now we were definitely more concerned. Everyone was trying to find out more about the war."

"I was a young mother, and I was very upset about the call-up," Betty McClure relates. "I hadn't followed the buildup in Vietnam. I hadn't paid too much attention to the fighting that was going on over there. I only saw a little on the evening news, and then not often.

"All this just swirled around us," she says. "We were sort of insulated, like living in the eye of a hurricane."

But after the call-up, her perspective changed dramatically.

"I took a lot more interest in the war, [in] things that were going on around us, out in the world," she says.

As soon as word of the call-up spread, the telephone at the

McClure home began to ring. It rang for two straight days as Guardsmen, their wives, girlfriends, parents called to find out if what they heard was true.

"The phones were really burning all over town that night," McClure remembers. But all he could tell the callers was that the men were to report to the armory on May 13 and would be sent to Fort Hood, Texas. He had no other information that night, April 11.

"All of the men have been through basic training," he said. "The training we'll get in Texas will be advanced unit training."

Many of the men in the unit had farm backgrounds, and that didn't allow you to put on excess weight.

"I'd say, by and large, everyone was in pretty good shape, except when it came to running a mile," remembers Don Parrish, a member of the Guard unit. "Running a mile will kill you, if you're not used to it."

"One hundred and twenty men and a multitude of problems" is the way McClure describes the situation a few days after the call-up.

"Two or three of the men are still trying to make up their minds if they want to qualify for that extra hundred and ten dollars a month," he says, meaning did they want to marry immediately, or wait until the battery returns. But one look at the social pages of the *Kentucky Standard* on April 18 told you what most of the young people had decided: marriage immediately, if not sooner.

Several women, some of them pregnant, would have to move back to Bardstown and live with relatives. Their husbands would be leaving jobs with Ford and General Electric in Louisville that paid $700 a month in exchange for army wages of around $300 each month. Some would get less. A private first class who was single and had two years' service would get $179 a month.

"That, plus clothing, quarters, food, and something to do every day," McClure says, somewhat facetiously.

A day later, McClure learned that the call-up was for approximately twenty-four months. "We'll probably do some processing - here, with the men reporting to the armory every day, and returning home each night," he added. McClure and four men went on active duty on Monday, April 18, to begin the processing. "I've ordered up eight more men for next week," he said. The rest of the battery will report to the armory on May 13, when the game changes from weekend warrior to regular army.

McClure asked local employers to allow the men to take any sick leave or vacation days they may be due to allow them to get their personal affairs in order.

"We may lose a few men from our authorized strength of one hundred twenty because some may not pass the physical and there may be a few hardship cases," McClure said in a newspaper interview. Of the 117 enlisted men in the battery, 105 lived in the Bardstown area and 12 lived outside Nelson County. Both officers, McClure and Ice, lived in Bardstown. There was an opening for a third officer that was yet to be filled. Three men whose enlistments were up before December 12 would not have to go.

Some of the men were in college. Some had just started new businesses. Only thirty-five of the men were single. The other eighty-five were married, many with young children. "We cannot take dependents with us at the present time, possibly later on," McClure said.

"The call-up will hurt," he added.

The men in the battery trained one weekend each month and spent fifteen days during the summer away at camp.

The date the unit would leave for Fort Hood, how long it would train in Texas, if it would eventually go to Vietnam, no one knew. "We have no definite word," McClure said. "Perhaps we'll know more in a day or so." The only thing he knew for certain was that the unit will leave its aging, outdated equipment behind—six howitzers and the vehicles that towed them—and will receive new gear when it arrives in Texas.

The units in the Kentucky battalion are the Headquarters and Headquarters Battery and Service Battery, both from Louisville; Battery A from Carrolton, Battery B from Elizabethtown, and Battery C from Bardstown. The 138th Artillery is based at the National Guard armory in Louisville. It is commanded by Lt. Col. Robert W. Cundiff, of Hodgenville.

"The Bardstown unit has been in the Selected Reserve Force for nearly two years," McClure said, "with all equipment and manpower at one hundred percent of readiness, and number-one priority for almost five years." Translated, this means that Battery C was one of the top-rated artillery outfits in the army, which a lot of the men found hard to believe, particularly because for the last several months they had been practicing riot control and had had no artillery training since the previous summer at camp.

A few of the Guardsmen said they expected to be called up that summer, but for duty in the big cities that were plagued with racial disturbances and antiwar demonstrations. No one dreamed he would be in a combat zone, under enemy fire, in several months.

"It [the battalion] has been concentrating on riot control training, and has been forced to neglect its conventional training," said Colonel Cundiff, the battalion commander.

"There is some catching up to do," he admitted, "and we need refresher training at the unit level."

Simply put, it was a Guard unit trained for riots that had been called for war.

Mary Nalley was selling women's clothing in a department store in Bardstown when Deanna Durbin came in and said, "Mary, have you heard?"

"Heard what?"

"The guys are going . . . they're going to be sent . . ." She didn't finish the sentence. She was very excited, perhaps a bit confused. But Mary knew what she meant.

"You've got to be kidding."

"No," Deanna said. "I just heard it."

Mary's boyfriend, Wayne Collins, was at work in Louisville at the time, so she couldn't reach him.

"It was a holy day, and I'm Catholic," Mary remembers, "so I went to church that night, and I still hadn't had a chance to talk to him." But when the service was over and she came out of church, Wayne was standing there, waiting. By this time, he had heard the awful news.

"We just rode around town, and talked," Mary says, "and we

decided that we would go ahead and get married." So they moved the date from July 2 to April 26, and became one more in an assembly line of marriages. Elizabeth Spalding, the editor of the *Kentucky Standard*, remembers that sad moment in Bardstown's history, and says, "I think we were a little bit overwhelmed when our Guard unit was called up. It brought the war a lot closer than it had been."

Three young men from the Bardstown area had been killed in Vietnam so far—Raymond Ford, William Russell Taylor, and William David Price—and Elizabeth Spalding says she could detect a change, however slight, in the feeling of the people toward the war. She could tell by listening to people at meetings, at luncheons, in her office, that they were becoming more interested in what was happening in Vietnam, and why.

"I think they began to say, 'Well, what is this all about? If we're not getting in there to win, what are we doing there?' "

"Not fighting the spread of communism? To my mother, that would be unthinkable," says Don Parrish, a member of Battery C. "To her, it would be like watching your house burn and not calling the fire department."

"In 1968, most of the people were still patriotic over the Vietnam war," former Mayor Gus Wilson remembers. "I would say, too, that about this time, our attitude began to change a little. A lot of 'em, like me, said, 'Well, it appears that our government has deceived us,' so their attitudes began to change."

———

Libby Hibbs was at home, playing with her newborn daughter, Jeri Gayle, when she heard on television that the Guard unit had been called up. The garage her husband, Ronnie, owned was across the street. He heard the bad news on the radio.

"I took off runnin' toward the garage as soon as I heard it," Libby recalls. "He took off runnin' toward the house," she says, "and we met in the middle of 480 Solitude Road."

"Oh, my God, what are they talkin' about?" she asked him.

"I don't know."

Ronnie and Libby ran into the house, he called the armory.

No one there knew anything other than that it was true, the unit had been called up. Their phone started to ring then because the men, as soon as they found out, began calling others to see what they knew. At this moment, rumors were the name of the game.

"Report to the armory."

"Don't report to the armory at this time."

"Get your gear together."

"Get your life in order."

"We're going on riot control duty."

"Take care of all the details."

"Talk to any PFC if you want to hear a rumor," McClure said at the time.

That night, some of the men got together to discuss the situation. Then they went to the armory.

"This can't be true," Libby recalls thinking. "There's something wrong here. I kept thinking that maybe they won't have to go, that maybe there's been a mistake.

"Then Ronnie came home and gave us the details," Libby says. Yes, the unit had been called up. There was no mistake. The men would report to the armory on May 13 to go on active duty. That was the extent of the details at that time.

———

Kent and Holly Bischoff, engaged at the time of the call-up, will never forget the day.

"Kent called me and told me about it," she remembers. "Then he came over to my house, where we had a little more privacy, and we talked."

"We're gonna go ahead and get married," Holly told him.

"I don't know if that's the right thing to do, to marry someone, and then go off and leave that person," he replied.

Since the call-up came on Holy Thursday, Kent, who was Catholic, and Holly, who was not, went to Mass that evening. Holly was preoccupied with thoughts of the future. What would the call-up mean for them? For their plans to marry in July?

"That night at Mass, I cried, and I cried, and I could not get control of myself," Holly recalls. "I remember thinking to myself, 'Gee, people are really gonna think I'm in the spirit of this Mass.'

"After that night, I did get some control over myself, but I do remember sittin' in church and really cryin'. From then on, I cried twice a day, every day, for six weeks," Holly adds.

It took them two weeks to resolve the dispute over their getting married. "We went through this struggle for a while," Holly says, "and I enlisted all the troops—his brothers and sisters, sister-in-law, everybody. They were all in agreement with me that we should go ahead and get married.

"So he finally consented, and we decided that we would get married on May fourth," she says.

Holly remembers the summer before, when the boys came home from camp. At that time, they had been ranked as one of the best artillery outfits, if not *the* best outfit, in the country.

"Kent was so proud of that, they were all very proud, but I remember saying to him, 'All you're gonna do is get yourself in trouble with that. Why couldn't you have muffed it a little bit?' "

———

At the time of the call-up, Betty Stone was in a hospital in Louisville, having just given birth to a son. Her husband, Charles, worked at the Ford plant there. He heard about the call-up on the radio and told his wife in her hospital room.

"I couldn't believe it," Betty says. "I don't think I fully absorbed it at that time." She left the hospital a few days later, and by then, it was beginning to sink in. "He would be gone in thirty days," she knew. "Maybe to Vietnam, and he would soon be in the regular army for a period of two years.

"So we moved back to Bardstown and moved in with my parents," she says. "Thirty days went by in a hurry. We got his uniforms together. Sewed on his patches. Said good-bye to friends. Tried to get our affairs in order. There just wasn't enough time to do what had to be done.

"He had to be at the armory every day to fill out papers for this, papers for that, have his medical records updated, get his shots, identification cards," she explains.

"When I took the baby to the doctor for the six-week checkup, my husband was upset because he couldn't go," she remembers. "He had to be at the armory.

"For the first time, I could see how this [the call-up] was going to affect our lives."

———

Don Parrish joined the Guard in 1964 at the age of twenty-two for a number of reasons—to satisfy his military obligation without taking two or three years out of his life, to stay home so he could remain close to the family business, and it seemed like the fun thing to do at the time because several of his friends were in the unit.

"My mother was very relieved that I was in the Guard, because she felt that I wouldn't be going off to war, or into battle somewhere," he recalls.

When the battery was called up, Parrish felt the unit might be going to Cincinnati, where trouble threatened. "I thought we'd be keeping the whites and the blacks from killing each other," he says.

"I had no idea I'd ever wind up in Vietnam," he continues. "Looking at the past history of Guard units, I had no idea that we'd ever go there. . . ."

But as soon as he had a chance to talk to Pat Simpson, the first sergeant put him straight, telling him that Vietnam was very definitely in his future.

———

Life was good for Mozena Cecil. She taught the third grade at St. Gregory's School. She enjoyed life in Bardstown. Same faces. Same houses. Nothing new. You could take a walk at night and not worry. Lots of friends. People helped each other if they needed it. She was comfortable there.

"I can't ever remember a door being locked in our house," she says.

Best of all, she was going to be married in June, just several weeks away, to Tom Raisor.

"I [had known] who Tom was," she says, "but we actually met one day in 1965 when I was driving down the highway and Tom was driving a truck carrying a load of doors and they all fell off and almost hit my car.

"My folks didn't say much about the war in Vietnam," she remembers. "They more or less accepted it, but they, the older people here, felt it was our duty to answer the call, to serve in Vietnam even if we didn't agree with it. It was an obligation.

"Vietnam was always somewhere else," she continues. "Chicago, New York, Los Angeles. But not here. It hadn't reached Bardstown yet.

"I wasn't interested in what was happening elsewhere. Just in my little area. I certainly wasn't ready to join a peace march.

"I think that Tom felt that the war was useless, that it was a waste," she adds.

"We really didn't talk too much about the war until the call-up, then we didn't talk about much else."

Raisor usually helped out on the family farm in the morning, then drove to his job in Louisville on the second shift at the General Electric plant. "After lunch, we'd usually sit around and watch the news on television for a while. Well, this particular day we heard, '. . . the 138th Artillery has been called up for active duty . . .'

"I couldn't believe what I had heard, so I called the armory and talked to Pat Simpson, and he confirmed it, saying, 'It's true, we've been called up.'

"I really didn't believe we were going," he remembers. "Maybe it was an alert. Maybe we were going to receive more specialized training."

As soon as he could get to a telephone, he called Mozena. She was in the school office when the phone rang.

"Our Guard unit has been called up," he told her.

"I was stunned, shocked, in a state of disbelief," she remembers. "I just couldn't believe it."

"How can they call you up?" she asked him.

It wasn't long before a lot of people were asking that same question, including many of the Guardsmen from the two batteries in Louisville, some from Battery C, and a few from Batteries A and B. Later, some of the parents became involved, and an attorney was retained to take the matter through the judicial system. The key issue was whether Guardsmen could be sent overseas because article 1, section 8, of the Constitution specifies that the militia can be called up only to "execute the laws of the Union, suppress insurrection, and repel invasions."

After talking to Tom, Mozena ran outside and shouted at Joanne Filiatreau, another teacher and a close friend.

"I told her what Tom said, that they had been called up, and then we both cried."

As soon as they could, Tom and Mozena got together and went over their plans to marry in June. "The first thing we did was put the wedding off," Mozena says, "because I don't think Tom thought he was going to come home."

━━━━━━

Sam Filiatreau was taking a nap on his lunch break at the Ford plant in Louisville when his foreman, Bob Norman, tapped him on the shoulder and woke him up, then asked: "Are you in the National Guard unit, the 138th Artillery?"

"Yes, I am."

"You're activated."

"It was just disbelief," Filiatreau remembers.

When he got home that night, Sam and his wife, Joanne, talked more about making the payment on the new house, the other bills, and their two young children than they did about the possibility of his going to Vietnam.

"We weren't concerned about Vietnam," he says. "I don't even think we talked about it, really."

"Well, I think it was always in your head, but it's just not something that we dwelt on," Joanne adds.

"If I had been waiting for the draft, I would have been much more concerned than I was," he explains. "But I was secure in the fact that I was in the Guard unit, and I thought I was protected— that I didn't have to worry about it.

"I would say that most of the people felt secure that they wouldn't go to Vietnam because they were in the Guard. In fact, I don't know of anybody that was at all worried about being called up.

"I remember that in 1962, the local reserve unit was activated for a crisis in Berlin, but they went to Fort Hood and stayed there the whole time. So I didn't feel like we were going to Vietnam, I really didn't.

"I wasn't anti-Vietnam, but I didn't particularly want to go there, either," he says. "But I felt patriotic. I felt that it was our duty to be there. I felt that it was our turn, and rather than try to get out of it, I was resolved to go, if I had to."

For that reason, he never became involved in the legal action that was developing in an effort to prevent the Guard unit from being sent overseas.

"I do know that there was a lot of resentment by people who were being drafted toward [men in] the National Guard and reserve units; they were getting the reputation of being draft dodgers," Filiatreau said.

At that time, regular army people often referred to National Guardsmen as "NG"—meaning "not going."

—————

Mobilization of the battery was moving quickly, but not necessarily smoothly. There were just too many things to be done in too little time. By May 9, some 33 of the 120 men in the unit were on active duty preparing the battery for departure to Texas on May 13. Equipment belonging to the federal government had already been turned in and was on the way to Fort Knox for shipment to Fort Hood. Most of the battery's property belonging to the Kentucky National Guard had already been turned in and would be distributed to other Guard units in the state. There was still an opening in the battery for a third officer.

"Jerry was one of those activated early to handle the paper maze that goes with a call-up such as this," Joy Janes says, "and every morning, he was out in front of the armory as I drove by on the way to school, and we would wave to each other."

Then there were the personal problems. The call-up caught the whole town by surprise. And nowhere was it felt more than in the area of human relationships. The call-up wrought havoc in the marriage plans of many young couples.

Deanna Durbin had already picked out her wedding dress and dresses for her bridesmaids, for her August marriage to Ronnie Simpson. But the wedding announcements had not been printed yet, which made it simpler for her to change their plans. "When he got called up, we decided to get married in April, so I rearranged things in a week and on the twenty-sixth of April, we were married in St. Gregory's Church with about one hundred fifty people attending." Then they lived at his brother's house until Ronnie's unit left for Texas.

Cracks may have begun to appear in the support for the war, but the people of Bardstown still felt passionately about the men fighting it. On Thursday, April 28, the *Kentucky Standard* reprimanded the University of Kentucky for permitting an avowed communist, Herbert Aptheker, to speak on campus:

> . . . it doesn't make sense that while our American men are fighting and dying in the Far East to prevent the communists from taking over the small country of South Vietnam, a man who is a communist and publicly talking the communist line should address other young people at our tax-supported state university.
>
> One of the chief aims of the communists is overthrow of the government—yet a communist is permitted to address our university students. What other purpose would he have than to sway or influence them

to the communist thinking? And what good could come of it?

We certainly cannot see what the administration of the University of Kentucky is thinking about when such a think line is permitted. We're in sympathy with the protesting veterans, who know what war is and have great compassion for our men bearing arms.

Our fight against communists should be on all fronts—the home front as well as in Vietnam. Certainly, our men in uniform must have a let-down feeling . . .

. . . and let it be known that we consider a communist speaking at the University of Kentucky an insult to our fighting men in Vietnam, and we want no more of it.

To add to the growing chaos, there were so many marriages taking place the week after the call-up, you couldn't keep track of them.

"They used to put pictures in the *Kentucky Standard* of the girls that were getting married . . . , and there would be three or four of them each week, at most," Holly Bischoff remembers. "After the call-up, you opened the *Standard,* and there was a double page of wedding pictures."

The assembly-line marriages continued until just before the Guard unit left for Texas.

"Kent was in David Collins's wedding the night before we were to be married," Holly recalls. "In fact, we couldn't have a formal rehearsal because of that. But as soon as that wedding was over, we rushed in and tried to do a little rehearsing."

Young couples were getting married so fast that they didn't have time to change the church decorations. They'd just turn the white runners over, rearrange the flowers, and split the cost.

Three women got together, agreed on white gladiolus, divided the cost, and shared the flowers.

"Word spread that they were out of those little white runners that the florist brings, so it was kind of panic time," Holly remembers. "Thank God I didn't know anything about this at that time," she adds.

"Kent, who was an usher in the Collins's wedding the night before, made sure that the runner from that wedding was rolled up backwards so that when it was rolled out for our wedding the next day, it would be clean.

"I remember I had a question I wanted to ask Kent, but back then, you never called a boy, he called you, especially on your wedding day. But one of the ushers had way too much to drink the night before, and he had a fight with his girlfriend. He was supposed to meet the florist and help with the flowers. Well, I got to worrying that he wouldn't even remember there was a wedding, much less anything else. So I called Kent, and his sister answered.

" 'Oh, he's out in the field,' " she told me.

"Now, this was an hour before the wedding, and I was a wreck before. I was now an absolute total nervous wreck," Holly adds.

"Anyway, he nicked the top of his hand somehow, and he shows up in a white formal tux—the white jacket, the black pants, and a big piece of black electrical tape on the top of his hand." Anyway, it all worked out. The church was full. There was no problem with the flowers, and in the grand tradition of Kentucky, the wedding of Holly and Kent took place on Derby Day.

They had a three-day honeymoon, then Kent returned to work.

Another couple had their wedding reception in Texas at a McDonald's, and their wedding picture was taken under the golden arches.

"The weddings would usually start early Friday evening and go on all day Saturday. Mainly, what everybody was trying to do was work in a time with the priest," Patsy Collins says. "So many people were getting married that he was working overtime. So you had to work the couples in as close as you could, then have them out of there for the next couple. If you had Mass with the wedding, it would probably take about ninety minutes. If you didn't, it would probably take about fifteen or twenty minutes."

"As the day for their departure for Texas neared, I became very tense, very nervous, anxious, and very resentful," Joy says. "Quite a few couples had married, mostly those who had planned to get married that summer but moved their wedding dates up after the unit was called up.

"The day they left was graduation day at Nazareth, where I was going to school, and my job that day was to play the organ," she explains. "I met Jerry, our families, and the others, at the armory early that morning, and I cried and cried.

" 'If you think it's hard to watch your boyfriend go off to war,' Jerry's mother said to me, 'wait until you watch your son go off to war.'

"That got me," Joy remembers, "and it really gets me now when I think of it, because I have four sons." She also has two daughters.

"The truck convoy left at seven A.M., and then I went home and got ready for graduation, sobbing, trying to get his leaving out of my mind."

After their marriage May 4, Patsy and David Collins drove to Nashville, Tennessee, for a day, then to Kentucky Lake for two days. When they returned to Bardstown, they spent a weekend with his parents, a weekend with hers. "We just had a little time together, so we wanted to be alone. We didn't accept any invitations to parties and picnics," Patsy says.

After the unit left for Texas, Patsy went down there with a group of wives and girlfriends in a caravan of several cars and vans. "We stayed at a motel with a nice pool. We'd walk around during the day until the husbands came home, then we'd go out to dinner, or go swimming. We had so much fun that many of us decided to stay a second week.

"We spent two of the most wonderful weeks together in Texas," she remembers. "I was working for Conway Motors at the time. I called back and asked for a second week off, and I got it."

―――

"I will never forget the night that Tom left for Texas," Betty McClure says. "That's the only time I ever saw him cry.

"Tom went to tell his son, Michael, good-bye and kiss him good night. As he tucked him in, Michael asked, 'Will I ever see you again?'

"That was very, very hard on Tom," she remembers. "I was crying. Tears were streaming down my face. I left Tom there. I couldn't stand it."

Then Tom went downstairs, and they cried in each other's arms in what she described as "probably the most emotional moment of our lives.

"That's when it really sank in. That he would be gone for at least a year. That we would be alone. Maybe I would never see him again. I knew that he was going to Vietnam. Would he come back?"

"The best thing Bardstown could do for those in the Guard unit was to be supportive of those who remained behind," says historian Dixie Hibbs. "Times were difficult then. Some had signed papers to buy a house the same day they got word that they were going to be called up, that they would be going to war.

"Even if the people were beginning to feel it was a senseless war, a useless waste of manpower, we didn't want to say it," she adds, "because we didn't want to hurt the loved ones here."

After the men left for Fort Hood, Deanna Simpson waited six weeks, then drove to Texas to be with her husband over the Fourth of July weekend. "Ronnie said not to give up my job and move to Texas, like a lot of women did, because 'you might need that job later.' He was right.

"I stayed for a week in a motel, and that was the best week of my life," she says.

While she was there, her sister, Pat, married Donnie Allender. "She got married in my wedding dress, and I wore her bridesmaid's dress that she wore at my wedding."

Getting called up was tough for Kent Bischoff. Who was going to run his dairy business while he was away? Who was going to milk sixty-five cows in the morning and again later in the day? Who would do the chores that a dairy of that size requires? Certainly not his father. "I'll help you get started," Kent's father had told him when he was only eighteen. "I'll help you financially, son," he'd said, "but I'm never gonna put my foot in a dairy. I hate 'em."

About the time of the call-up, Kent's younger brother, Tom, got out of college and said he'd run the farm in Kent's absence. However, then Tom got drafted and faced the prospect of going to Vietnam. Back then, brothers didn't have to go to Vietnam unless they signed a waiver, and they didn't sign. But they talked it over and decided that since Kent was a sergeant, and in supply, he would stand much less chance of getting shot than Tom, who would have been a private and a good choice for the front lines. For some mysterious reason, though, Tom received several thirty-day delays, so his departure was put off. Then their neighbor stepped in and did all the work necessary to keep the dairy afloat. In Bardstown, everyone pitches in when someone needs help.

"Through a haze of tears, I watched the men at the armory as they left for Texas," Holly remembers. "I cried and waved good-bye." She was twenty and in college. With her husband gone for at least a year, she intended to go back for her senior year to earn her degree. But then she began having second thoughts.

"I thought, 'No, the best thing for me is to get pregnant, because if he never comes back from Vietnam, we'll always have something to remember him by.'

"I'd pray that this child would be exactly like him," she says. "Well, let me tell you, God listened. The only thing that is like me is her sex."

Tears were a big part of everyone's life then. Holly cried regularly twice a day. You could pretty much set your watch by her tears. This continued for a little more than three weeks, until Kent called with the good news: dependents were now welcome to join their husbands in Texas. So were girlfriends.

"Bobby Stumph and I have rented a duplex," Kent explained, "and you and Lorraine are gonna come down." Holly vaguely knew who Bobby and Lorraine were, and that they had a brand-new baby. But she wasn't too thrilled about the possibility of spending several months with them.

"Well, all right, I'll come down," she told her husband, "but you know, I just don't think I'm gonna like those people.

"She and I were very cautious of each other at first," Holly relates, "but the boys would take Kent's car to the base every day, which meant that she and I had to do everything together, so we became friends.

"She is one of the best friends I have, and I don't know what I would have done without her," Holly says. "Not everything about the war was terrible. My best friends came about as a result of associations in the Guard.

"Lorraine had this brand-new baby, and pretty soon I was expecting," Holly continues. "I have no brothers or sisters, so I didn't know anything about babies. But Lorraine nursed hers, so I nursed mine. I learned everything I know about raising kids from her.

"A lot of girls whose husbands had no rank, who were PFCs, had to live in abominable situations," Holly recalls. But Kent was a staff sergeant, which meant they got a little more money, could live a little better than the rest.

"We had this duplex," she says. "Now, I'm not saying it was the nicest duplex, but when you're young and you just got married, you don't care."

Holly and Lorraine arrived on a Sunday night. Their husbands had to be on base very early, six days a week.

"When Lorraine and I got up in the morning, we scrubbed, and we scrubbed, from floor to ceiling, all day long, and it didn't look any better than when we began scrubbing."

"After we finished cleaning, Holly painted her living room

aqua and her refrigerator, which seldom worked, gold," Lorraine remembers.

"What I'm trying to say is, when you're young and in love, with Vietnam hanging over your head, you think something like this is a wonderful place," Holly declares.

"I remember when Joy came down to visit Jerry," Holly says. "We put her on the sofa, then I kept an eye on her. We were all the same age, we'd been friends for years, and I felt like I was supposed to be their chaperone, I felt this awesome responsibility to her mother that I'd do these things right.

"I remember Joy going out with Jerry one night, and here I am asking her, 'What time do you plan to be back here?'

"Texas was a unique experience," Holly says, "because all these guys would come to our place all the time, because they had no place else to go.

"Actually, they were just a bunch of grown-up teenagers," she remarks.

One night, Holly and Kent were off to the drive-in, more to be alone than to see a movie. But halfway there, Kent remembered that he forgot the beer. "Heaven forbid, you'd go to the drive-in without your beer," Holly said. So they turned around and headed back home. "I didn't want to go back," Holly says. "I wanted an evening of privacy. You have to realize that I had to deal with these guys all the time. I was like a den mother, and I was younger than all of them.

"When we turned at the end of our street, I saw Jerry and six or seven other nuts, laying in our front yard," Holly recalls.

"Hurry, quick, let's get out of here," Holly said to Kent, and ducked, hoping no one would see them. Too late.

"Hey, there's Bish!" Jerry shouted.

"Too late," Kent said. "They saw us."

"Hey, Bish, c'mon, you got company," Jerry shouted at them.

"So we backed up, and I wish you could have seen them," Holly says. "You could see that they'd already had plenty of beer. They were the filthiest bunch of men I had ever laid my eyes on."

They'd been drinking in a restaurant when one of them asked another to pass the butter. Rather than pass it, he threw it. Then the bread flew through the air. Soon a full-fledged food fight erupted.

Then the police were called. One of the guys picked up a rare steak and hit another one in the face, and they ran out the back door. Jodie Haydon jumped into a garbage can to hide. Jerry Janes ran into it, and Jodie rolled out. "People in Texas are gonna talk about us if you boys don't straighten up," she told them.

"I got 'em inside and tried to clean 'em up," Holly relates. "They had baked potatoes in their hair. Jerry had on another guy's shirt, and it was covered with steak sauce and what comes out of a very rare steak."

Holly recalls another story. "One Sunday, they were all there, some of 'em watching football on my TV, some of 'em watching Glen Campbell on Lorraine's TV. I walked in, and Jodie was sitting on my thirty-eight-dollar recliner, and one of them was just pumping catsup on his head. It was all over the place.

"Jodie never moved, he never blinked," she says.

"I thought I was bleeding to death," he says.

And another story. "One morning, I noticed an unusual number of cars driving by our place," Holly says. "They'd be driving at normal speed, then when they'd get to our house, they'd slow way down. So Lorraine and I went out on the porch, but didn't see anything."

"What in the world is going on?" Holly asked her.

"Holly, I don't know."

Since everyone was still looking at their house, they walked out to the street and turned around.

"The fools—they'd come over the night before, brought their own steaks and beer, and had a party," Holly explains.

By the time they were finished, they had enough empty beer cans to cover the roof. And that's what they did. They covered the roof with the empty cans. "There were hundreds of 'em up there," Holly says. "We couldn't get up there to get 'em down, so we had to wait until the boys got home that night.

"If you met the boys today, you'd never believe they could do some of the things they did then. They're so straight, so prim and proper," she adds. "They were just letting off steam. They knew where they were going. That their lives would be in peril. That maybe some of 'em wouldn't be coming back.

"The sheriff's sister lived across the street from us, and I don't know if she called and told him about the beer cans, but I know we didn't make a big hit with the local authorities," Holly says.

One afternoon, Holly and Lorraine went out in the front yard to get some sun. Holly had on a two-piece bathing suit, nothing indecent. Not long after that, they both began to receive strange phone calls.

"We know you're there, alone," the caller would say.

"We were both quite frightened," Holly says. "So Lorraine called the sheriff's office and told them about the calls."

"Well, if you women wouldn't lay around in the yard in your swimsuits, you wouldn't have this trouble," she was told.

"Those guys, they drank a lot of beer, and once in a while, driving down those country roads, they'd hit a cow," Holly adds. "So I don't think the authorities were on our side."

———

Joy Brooks and Mozena Cecil flew down to Texas together and checked into adjoining rooms in a motel in the quaint little town of Killeen to be with their boyfriends, Jerry Janes and Tom Raisor, respectively. But sometimes the best laid plans just don't work out. Mozena had to return to Bardstown unexpectedly because of a death in the family. Joy wound up spending more time with her friend, Holly, than with Jerry, because the men were in the field most of the time.

So Joy moved in with Holly and Kent Bischoff in their half of the duplex. "Jerry was upset because he made plans for me to come down, then he had to spend most of the time in the field," Joy remembers.

"But Holly and I had become good friends by this time, so we kept ourselves busy by going to the Laundromat and shopping for groceries. I know that sounds silly now, but it was fun then, because she was newly married, and things like cooking supper and decorating the little apartment were interesting to us. And just being down there was fun.

"Holly and Kent had a convertible, so it was fun cruising around in that," she adds.

"I don't have too many memories of being with Jerry in Texas, because he was in the field most of the time," Joy says.

"Training kept the men busy, which they liked, because the time went by much faster. They fired their howitzers, machine guns, grenade launchers, and hurled live hand grenades. All in a day's work. When they weren't in the field, it was softball, the men who lived on base versus those who lived off base."

But soon the steady flow of wives to join their husbands had an effect on the softball games as more and more men moved off base. "This barracks has been becoming more and more deserted," Don Parrish wrote in a letter to the *Kentucky Standard*, "and nights are not quite as full of excitement now as they used to be, and there are promises of more wives yet to come.

"Pretty soon the remainder of the Battery [on base] will be able to move into one small room, and [we can] close the rest of the barracks down."

Most of the women stayed down there for three months and then returned to Bardstown when the unit came back for thirty days' leave.

"I didn't want to come back," Joy remembers. "I wanted to stay there with the rest of them. There was a junior college close by, and I thought of transferring, but that would have created too many problems." So she returned home.

"With Jerry being gone, I see it as a year out of our lives," Joy says. "I felt like we were being denied a part of our natural growth.

"I had a great feeling of resentment. Why did it have to be me? This feeling would come and go, and it really wasn't a good feeling. I was very upset that our lives had to be put on hold for who knows how long.

"We really didn't know if we'd be picking up our lives," she adds. "Something could happen to Jerry. I was very upset. Then I'd calm down and tell myself, 'This is just something we have to go through. We're not the first. And there will be others. This will make us better people.' Then I'd start counting the days until his return.

"You know, at times I was back and forth so far as the war was concerned. At times I'd look at it from a selfish standpoint and wonder, 'Why did we have to sacrifice—it was the best time of our lives.'

"At other times I could accept it as our role in history," she adds.

"I teach music and English literature today, and when my students ask me about the war, I tell them it was our responsibility to go, to get involved, just like it was our responsibility to get involved in Korea and World War II."

Mary Collins was living with her parents while the Guard unit was in Texas. She was still working at the clothing store. She also had a government paycheck coming in now. And she was making all the decisions for herself and Wayne. "But if there was a big, really important decision to be made, I'd write him, and then we'd discuss it," she explains.

"He had just gone to Fort Hood, and I missed him already," she says. "I guess I missed him before he even left."

She was at her parents' home one evening, and the phone rang. It was Wayne.

"I want you to come to Texas," he told her.

"Well, what about my job?"

"Forget about that," he said. "Just come to Texas."

"So I did," she said. "I took a leave of absence and stayed there for three months, and I never regretted it."

"Saying good-bye to my husband was a sad, tearful few minutes," Libby Hibbs remembers. "It was really sad."

"I love you," she told him as they embraced. "Be careful down there."

"I love you, too," Ronnie told her. "Take care of yourself while I'm gone."

"There were tears everywhere, not just us," she says. "All the wives and girlfriends were crying. It was one of the saddest moments I can remember."

Then they parted at the armory when the men boarded vehicles that would take them to the airport in Louisville and their flight to Texas.

Her husband's partner, who had kept their small body shop open during the thirty days before the unit left, then closed the business. Libby, who had an infant daughter, Jeri Gayle, stayed at her home during the day, and at her parents' home at night. "We lived in the country, and they didn't want me to be alone," Libby explains.

Almost as soon as he had left, she began to think about going down there to be with him, but she didn't know if he would be able to find a place for them to live. And they had an infant. Libby didn't know anyone from Bardstown, until the men got called up. She met some of the women at the armory that day. A short time after the men were gone, the wives and girlfriends started calling each other, offering support, to see if anyone needed help of any kind.

"This was all new to me," Libby says. "Then we all began calling each other to find out who was going to Texas. We'd just talk on the phone. They all knew each other. I didn't."

"When my husband got down there, he was able to find a house in Lampasas, about thirty miles from Fort Hood," Libby says.

"So I drove to Texas with my baby in a cardboard box, and a woman by the name of Sandy Shelburne was with me. [Driving] behind me was a young woman by the name of Judy Raymond, who didn't even have a driver's license.

"I remember one time I looked in the rearview mirror and saw that Judy had driven off the road, and then swung sharply back on the road, in the process doing a complete turn, a three-sixty," Libby recalls.

"She liked to scared me to death," she adds.

The house in Texas had two bedrooms. Since her husband knew all the men in the unit, they would often come home with him. One time, Wayne Collins showed up.

"He remarked that Mary, his wife, was coming, and they needed a place to stay. In fact, he said, Mary was arriving that very same day," Libby recalls.

"Wayne got in touch with her, told her where he was, and when she arrived, it was instant liking," Libby relates. "I told them there was no need to find a place. They could stay with us.

"Mary was pregnant then and pretty sick at times," Libby says, "so I helped take care of her as best I could.

"We became very good friends," she adds.

"One day, Mary asked if I'd like to go up to Killeen to meet a friend of hers, Betty Stone. Later, when the guys were in the field overnight, Mary and I would stay with Betty."

"Mary kind of took care of me," Libby continues. "She knew everyone. She was like a mother to me.

"When we got together, we'd go shopping. And talk. There was a lot of talking going on down there, believe me."

When the men were training, the women would often get together at big, beautiful Lake Benton, which was a few miles away. "We'd go there to eat and talk and try to figure out if the guys were really going to Vietnam, or someplace else," Libby remembers.

They'd picnic. Go swimming. All the kids were there. Under the circumstances, they had a good time.

"We tried to enjoy ourselves and not think about the circumstances that brought us together in Texas, why we were there," Libby explains.

"We talked about a lot of things simply to keep our minds off what was always on our minds: our husbands were probably going to Vietnam," she adds.

"But even then, we still held out a little hope that something would happen, that they wouldn't be going overseas."

Betty Stone remembers the six-car caravan of women that made that fifteen-hour trek to Texas so they could be with their husbands.

"My dad was very protective," she says. "He didn't want me going down there alone, driving, so Mary Collins went with me, and my brother, Ronnie, drove." Five other cars followed.

"It was a sad, somber group of women that drove to Texas," she remembers. "I had our baby, then six weeks old, in a dresser drawer, and Mary was pregnant, Lorraine Stumph had her new baby with her, several others had babies with them, one woman got sick, several were expecting.

"It was quite an experience," she remarks. "We were all very young, in our early twenties. I don't think any of us could have handled it alone. We needed each other to lean on. We needed support from each other.

"It was a very sad time in our lives," she adds.

Most of the women stayed in Killeen, a modest-size army town adjacent to sprawling Fort Hood, the largest military post in the free world. A few went to nearby Copperas Cove, and a few drove on to Lampasas, about thirty-five miles from Killeen. Betty shared a house with David Stone, a cousin, his wife, Pam, and a daughter, Jennifer, about a year and a half old.

Killeen is an old town, going all the way back to 1882, and was named after Frank J. Killeen, who brought the first railroad there so that great quantities of cotton, grain, and wool could be shipped east. But in the early days of World War II, the military at Fort Hood became the source of Killeen's livelihood.

If you visited Killeen but never saw Fort Hood, you couldn't help noticing a military presence somewhere in the area just by the neatly trimmed hair. Today, Killeen is a totally service-oriented community. When the 340 square miles of Fort Hood thrives, so does Killeen. But when the base declines, so does Killeen's economy. Killeen's population averages sixty-eight thousand, depending on the activity at the base. The town and the base are so closely related, in fact, that if you walk out the east gate, you're in Killeen. But the railroad no longer plays a big role in the town's livelihood, and the old train station now houses the chamber of commerce.

Killeen saw many tears, and sad farewells, from World War II and Korea. Vietnam was no different.

The women tended to the households. They cared for the children. Cleaned. Went shopping. Cooked. "We more or less stayed together to talk, to bolster each other's morale," Betty Stone says.

They were frightened, too, particularly at night.

"When our husbands were out training, then Mary and Libby would come over to our house so we could be close together," Betty recalls, "then we'd talk and sort of take care of each other.

"It seems like we were always waiting for the men to come home," she remembers.

"Our home down there was always open to the guys," Betty

says, "particularly those who were alone, whose wives couldn't come, or who had to return to jobs after spending a week or two there, whose girlfriends couldn't make the trip."

The wives had been in Texas with their husbands for about three and a half months, and now it was time to go home, to pack up and return to Bardstown. Circumstances being what they were, it had been a pleasant summer for most of them. They became well acquainted. Libby Hibbs, for instance, who hadn't known anyone from Bardstown, now had friends she could count on for help. Adversity had seen them grow closer together. The summer had been hot and humid, and they didn't have air-conditioning. Great windstorms. Hail the size of golf balls. And the rain, thunder, and lightning.

"Unless you've been in a Texas cloudburst, you haven't seen heavy rain," Betty Stone says. "Sometimes it rained so hard, you couldn't go anywhere, not even to the store."

But there had been wonderful times, too. Sometimes just talking helped them over the rough spots. Now it was back to Bardstown, and an uncertain future. Certainly loneliness. Sadness. Worry. New responsibilities. Making all the decisions for husbands who would be away at war for at least a year. Having children. Raising families alone. Handling the money. And fear. Would all the men return? This was a delicate subject, one that was not discussed openly, but one that was on the minds of everyone.

But there were indicators throughout the summer that the men would eventually end up in Vietnam, and that to think otherwise would be unrealistic.

For instance, one Sunday, Joy Brooks got a call from Jerry Janes, who told her, "Well, we got our fatigue underwear, you know, the green underwear." Obvious sign that the jungle was in their future, that they soon would be called to war.

"So we knew that there was no hope, despite the lawsuit," she says.

"Yeah, we did hold out hope because of the lawsuit," Holly Bischoff adds. "That was the last carrot hanging out there."

But as much as the women missed Bardstown, they all realized going home was a giant step toward Vietnam for their men.

A month's leave may seem like a long time, but when you may

never see each other again, it becomes very brief. For Joy Brooks and Jerry Janes, it was a very difficult time. "We were dating, and then eleven-thirty came, we'd have to say good night," she remembers. "That's when it really hit you, made you realize that the days were coming to an end, that they'd be gone soon."

At one gathering, she remembers telling Jerry, "It is not possible, it is not realistic to think that all of you will come back, is it?"

"No," Jerry replied, "it isn't."

"Then I looked out over the crowd, thinking, 'The next time we get together, who will not be here?'"

While the men were home on leave, Don Parrish wanted to buy an attractive piece of property just outside of town. "I went to the bank and talked to the bank president, wanting to get a loan from him to buy this piece of property. I think it was gonna be like seven thousand dollars."

"Well, I can't loan you money for that," the banker told him. "You may get killed in Vietnam, and I wouldn't be able to get my money back."

While they were home, a large number of the men attended a gathering in Louisville to back the legal effort that was moving slowly through the courts to halt their shipment to Vietnam. The battalion commander, Lt. Col. Robert Cundiff, was there, too, and told the men, "I feel that we were called to do a job as responsible men. Whether it's legal or not is for somebody else to decide."

The call-up, he added, "was the breaks of the game," and the publicity the group was receiving would be damaging to the battalion.

"Enjoy your vacations, and I'll be looking forward to seeing you at Fort Hood," the colonel concluded.

When the time came to say good-bye, the partings were brief, and tear-filled, whether they were in Kentucky or Texas.

Patsy Collins saw her husband, David, for the last time at the airport in Louisville.

"I love you, I love you so much," he told her.

"I love you, too," she told him, her face wet with tears.

"I'll be back, I'll be back," he said, again and again. "The year will be over before we know it, and we'll be together again."

"There were tears everywhere," Patsy remembers. "There were couples, families on both sides, and everyone was crying."

"I remember him leaving the armory and going back to Texas," Deanna Simpson says of her husband, Ronnie, whom she never again saw. "We hugged, and I cried."

"Be careful, I miss you already," she whispered. "Write every day."

"You, too. I love you," he told her.

"I love you, too."

"We still held out a little hope that our husbands wouldn't be going to Vietnam," Libby Hibbs remembers, "but deep in our hearts, I guess we really knew they'd be going."

The men went back to Fort Hood to pack their gear, the big equipment, trucks, communications, the new and powerful M-109 tracked 155 howitzers that carried a crew of ten, in two shifts of five each. They also brought personal equipment not normally sent to a battle zone—three ice makers, one large freezer, twelve refrigerators, and five washing machines—that the people of Bardstown sent them.

On the way to Texas, Parrish and Jim Moore, a member of the battery, sat next to each other. Moore remarked, "We're probably just going to fly out over the ocean, turn around, and come back. You know, this is probably all part of a big training maneuver."

"No, Jim, we're going to where the action is," Parrish told him.

Libby and her baby flew down to Texas to be with her husband, Ronnie, for the last two weeks, until the men shipped out on October 21 for Vietnam. She stayed at a motel close to the base, and they spent as much time together as they could.

Then it was good-bye.

"When I left to come back, Lord, it was sad," she remembers, "and I cried and cried."

"I love you, I love you. Please be careful and write. Be sure and write every day," she told him, her eyes clouded by tears.

"I love you, too. I'll write you every day, and you write, too," he said.

"It was terrible," Libby says. "I knew I wouldn't see him for at least a year, maybe I wouldn't see him again.

"On the way back to Kentucky, the baby cried, and I cried and cried. People on the plane were wondering what was the matter. A woman, a stranger, tried to help me. Then the baby began to cry more, because she was upset that I was crying. It was awful.

"Between the baby and me, we cried enough to do a laundry," Libby adds.

Betty Stone and Mary Collins drove back to Texas to be with their husbands for those last two weeks. Betty had her baby. Mary was pregnant, but not as sick as she was during the early weeks of her three-month stay.

"It was a wonderful stay in Texas," Betty remembers. "Just being alone was wonderful, yet it was sad, too, because we knew in a few days we would be leaving, and they would be going to Vietnam.

"It was a sad, tearful good-bye," she recalls, "because we really didn't know if we'd see them again. I guess that was always in the back of our minds.

"Coming home from Texas the second time was the worst part of my life," Betty says. "It was terrible. I wasn't sure I was going to make it." The two women tried to talk about anything that would distract them from thoughts of the war. It didn't work. They tried to help each other over the rough moments by being good listeners. Although it helped, the tears were always there.

"For some reason, my mother let me fly back to Texas to say good-bye to Jerry," Joy Brooks remembers. "Later, I asked her why she let me go back the second time, and she said, 'Well, it was cheaper than burying you. If I didn't let you go down and say good-bye, I was afraid you were gonna die.'" Their two weeks sped by, and before anyone realized it, the time had come to part.

"You know, you've got a year now. You've got to make the best of this year so that all the years that follow will be good years," she told Jerry at the little airport in Killeen. She got on the plane, her seat was by the window, and she saw Jerry just as he gave her a great big good-bye wave. The flight attendant saw that she was about to burst into tears, and brought her a glass of water. "I cried so hard on leaving that I had to put my sun glasses on," Joy remembers, "but I had to take them off so often to dry my eyes that I just finally left them off."

The last few days before the men were to leave for Vietnam wasn't all sadness and tears, though. Holly and Kent Bischoff had a room at a motel just outside Fort Hood. Again, she was the den mother, trying to keep an eye on the wild bunch. Another couple had the room next door. The guys were drinking beer and watching a football game. Then someone turned on a tape recorder. "You can imagine the language when a bunch of army guys with too much beer are watching a football game, and hollering on every play," Holly remembers. "You never heard such language."

Then Jodie Haydon decided to make a tape and send it home to his mother. "You know, it was, 'Good-bye, Mom. I'll miss you so much, and if I never come back, you were the best mother ever and I'll never forget you.' You know, all that good-doin' stuff," Holly relates.

"Well, somehow they got the tapes mixed, and Jodie's mother got the one watching the football game and all the bad language," Holly says.

"Jodie's mother never thought he'd ever say a curse word for anything on the face of this earth," she adds. "Then she gets this tape with her son saying every curse word that's ever been invented, and a few of his own.

"Things like that kept us amused, kept our minds off what was just around the corner, Vietnam," Holly says. The other tape? It's still missing.

"We knew they were going to be leaving soon," Mary Collins remembers thinking during those last days in Texas, "but in the back of our minds we kept saying, 'No, something's gonna happen. They're not gonna go.'

"There was always a little bit of hope that this [going to Vietnam] was not gonna happen, that maybe they'd just fly out over the ocean, then come back, on an exercise, or that they'd fly to Korea, but not to Vietnam. That's not what the National Guard was for."

The day before the Supreme Court was to consider their case, the army shipped Battery C to Vietnam. The next day, Justice William O. Douglas conceded that because the soldiers "have been spirited out of the country," the request to halt their movement was meaningless.

"After the men left for Vietnam, life did go on, although it was day by day," Mozena Raisor remembers. "The letters that came daily from Texas didn't come that often from Vietnam, and when they did come, we'd share them."

Life in Bardstown took on a new meaning for the young mothers, wives, girlfriends—one of great loneliness, and worry. The mailman became the most important person in town. Little things now took on an extra dimension, such as a minor car accident, or an illness, a cold. But adversity seemed to bring the women closer together, even though many of them had been close since childhood. Despite the hardship, life was easier for them than if they lived in a large city. There were so many friends to call on when one needed help, or a friendly ear to listen to problems.

"If someone didn't get a letter, we'd get together, talk and share our mail," Mozena says. "It was a big help and kept our morale up.

"There were about ten of us that were very, very close," she relates. "We'd go out together to the movies, shopping, lunch, anything that would help us forget." Much of the time, they'd just talk and listen, and it didn't make any difference if it was just gossip. "It helped take our minds off Vietnam," Mozena explains. "It was pretty lonely then, without the person you planned to spend the rest of your life with."

Her husband, Tom, had always been a rather quiet person, not inclined to talk too much about anything, certainly not Vietnam. His letters were heavily censored. About all he could say was that they had fired a lot of rounds, and that they were firing more each day. "From that, I gathered that he was in the thick of the fighting," his wife recalls. "While I didn't expect the worst, it was always in the back of my mind."

The women of Bardstown found that the best way to cope was to keep busy with school, various projects, their children.

For Joy Brooks, it was college. She'd get there about eight A.M., often staying until eight P.M. Then there was homework, and Nazareth College demanded a lot of that. She was also involved in extracurricular activities. Even so, she cried twice a day for a long time. "Usually, when there wasn't anything for you to do, that's when your mind started to work, when you began to think, and then the tears would come," she says.

"Letters from Jerry were very important, naturally, but I never let anyone read them, although I shared information with all the women," she explains. To pass the time, to help herself get through a particularly tough day, when thinking brought forth a flood of tears, she would play mind games with herself.

"I'd tell myself that maybe this will be the day that the war ends. And I'd stay up and watch the eleven-o'clock news. Then, when they played the 'Star-Spangled Banner' at midnight, I'd realize the day was gone and the war was not over. But by then, you were too tired to stay awake, so you'd fall asleep telling yourself that maybe tomorrow will be the day the war ends."

"Life was awful. I was lonesome and very sad," Libby Hibbs recalls. During the day, she and her baby lived in her home, but at night, she and the baby stayed with her parents because she lived in the country and was afraid to be alone after dark.

By now, her life consisted of spending time with her new friends, Mary Collins and Betty Stone, and others she had met after the call-up. "We'd get together and talk, share letters, share tapes and photographs," she says. "If you missed getting a letter for a day or two, then they would come in bunches," she adds.

"The mailman, Harry Brown, kept all my mail on the dash," she explains. "If he caught me at my home, he'd drop it there. If he saw me on the road, he'd flag me down and give it to me, or he'd drop it off at my parents' home."

"With the men gone, I felt very, very sorry for myself," Holly Bischoff says. "I thought I was the only person that had ever been put in this position, that I would have to bear a baby alone."

In Texas, the women were spread out, so they really didn't share the unity that they had grown up with in Bardstown. Now that they were all back home, that old feeling of unity surfaced.

"I didn't get a letter every day, but I, like most of the other women, got a letter for every day," she recalls.

"We had a really good network of women who would get together and share letters with those who didn't get one for a day or so," she says. "The guys were really good about putting everyone in their letters just for that purpose."

A few months later, Holly sent her husband a movie camera,

the cheapest one she could find, a Bell and Howell that you had to crank by hand. "The guy at the PX told me to do that, to buy the cheapest one with the most plastic parts," she says.

"Why?" she asked him.

"Because of the high moisture in Vietnam," he said. "If it has a lot of metal parts, it will corrode." Her husband sent back a lot of film. So did all the other men. The women would get together, bring all the film, a projector, and a screen, and go to a drive-in restaurant close by. They'd put the screen inside, show the film, and if anyone's husband was in it, they'd get on the phone and say, "Hey, we've got some film here, and your husband is in it," and that woman would come on down and watch it. The same with letters. If someone was mentioned in a letter, they'd call his wife or girlfriend and tell her about it.

"If Kent wrote me a letter and said that so and so's doing such and such, no matter how dumb it was, I'd get on the phone and tell that person's mother, wife, or sister," Holly says.

Pregnancies also brought the women close. "We all got pregnant about the same time," she says. "It was disgraceful how many baby showers I had. I think it was six. And I know I went to at least six others."

One night, Holly was playing cards with friends. The telephone rang. It was the long-distance shortwave operator.

"You have a call from your husband."

"I was delighted," she says. "I could hear him, faintly, so I started to talk.

" 'You ought to see me. I look like I swallowed a watermelon. I look as big as a rain barrel. . . .' Then I hear this guy in the middle say, 'Over. You ought to see me. I look like I swallowed a watermelon. . . . Over.' Then I hear Kent's voice, and another 'Over,' and the guy in the middle gives me Kent's answer.

"It was the most frustrating experience of my entire life," Holly remembers. "Here I have my husband on the line, and I can't talk to him.

"I felt absurd saying 'I love you,' because then I hear 'Over. I love you. Over.' Then Kent tells me he loves me, and I go through the same thing all over again.

"When I got off the phone, I started crying, and I must have cried for three or four hours. I sat in the bedroom, and the tears just flowed.

"I wrote him the next day, and I said, 'Don't ever call me again. That was horrible. It was so impersonal.' And he didn't. He never called me again."

Almost immediately, the letters began to flow between Deanna Simpson and her husband, Ronnie. He sent movie film back to her. She sent photographs to him. Frequently, the women got together to share letters, movies, tapes. "His letters became more important the longer he was gone, and I treasured them," she says.

"There were so many of us that were in the same situation, so we all stayed pretty close together," Mary Collins recalls. "We visited each other. A lot were pregnant. A lot were having babies. We made sure that we were there when someone needed us, needed some help.

"So far as our letters were concerned, we'd compare notes, fill in the blank spots," she explains. "If I heard something about someone else from Wayne, I'd call that person, his wife or his girlfriend, and tell her, and they'd do the same.

"The letters were a big part of our lives then, perhaps the biggest part, and we really looked forward to receiving them," Mary says. "We'd get three or four a week, usually, but sometimes the mail would get held up somewhere, and then we'd get four or five in a bunch.

"I remember one time that I had to leave town and go stay with an aunt who was ill. That was a very lonely time, because I didn't get a letter that entire week. I remember calling home a number of times and asking, 'Did I get a letter today?'

" 'Yes, they're waiting for you.' "

That was the most welcome news anyone in Bardstown could hope for.

Letters were just as important at the other end, in Vietnam, where the men of Battery C were about to experience the harshness of war. For some, a letter would be the last link with home.

THREE

A Bad Hill

The men had hardly settled in their seats on the giant transport that carried the last of Battery C from Texas to Vietnam before their minds began to wander, before the gears began to turn, but not necessarily mesh.

"A few of them were apprehensive," Don Parrish remembers. "Several still thought we'd just fly out over the ocean, turn around, and come home. Some actually believed this until we landed at Midway to refuel. Several others were looking for combat experience.

"I just wished the whole darn thing would go away, and so did many others," he adds.

They talked about everything on the long flight to the war. Nothing, or no one, was sacred.

"We wondered about what to expect in Vietnam, we reminisced about old times growing up together," Parrish says. "Several were recently married, and we talked about whether that was the thing to do." For twenty-two hours, they talked, slept, and worried. Finally, they could feel the plane begin to descend. Then two members of the flight crew came out and handed each man two clips for his M-16. "Put one in your rifle, the other in your pocket," the artillerymen were told. Then a message came over the intercom: "Immediately upon departure from the plane, be prepared to move to an area of safety, because there has been a rocket attack on the base." Then another member of the crew walked through and matter-of-factly explained, "Right now, there's nothing going on, but rocket attacks happen all the time. You just never know when. That's why you don't want to be caught in large crowds. So when you get off the plane, don't stay in groups—scatter, disperse, and someone will come get you."

Welcome to Vietnam.

"That was probably the scariest thing I heard the whole time I was there," Parrish says. The C-141 touched down at Da Nang at four A.M., and the men scattered.

"That first foot on the ground, that was really something," Parrish recalls. "It was really something to know that you were not on American soil. This was the first realization that it had happened, that we were in Vietnam, that this was not an exercise." It took about four days for all the men to get there to begin to organize.

"Are you convinced now that we're gonna wind up in Vietnam?" Parrish asked Ronnie Hibbs.

"Yeah, I'm sure in the hell sure," he replied.

At first light, the men boarded another plane and flew to Phu Bai, about seventy-five miles north of Da Nang, and the home of the 101st Airborne Division at Camp Eagle, an area of mass confusion, the outfit the artillerymen would support with their howitzers. In return, there would always be at least a platoon of infantry with Battery C for protection. They were at Camp Eagle for three days, then moved to Gia Lai, no more than loud shouting distance from the paratroopers. Camp Eagle was nice. Gia Lai was a little better. Both were training positions where you could ease yourself into the Vietnam atmosphere. As soon as the battery was together, they received an orientation, what to watch for, what to expect.

"Everybody's runnin' around in what they call pajamas, little short people, it was totally different," Tom Raisor remembers. "In my case, I guess I didn't know enough to be scared. If you've never been to a war zone, you don't know what to expect."

A briefing officer tried to point their heads in the right direction, tried to get them to look at Vietnam through the same set of eyeballs: watch the kids, they can be dangerous. They will throw a grenade in your jeep. Watch the civilians, they can be dangerous.

They found out where incoming heavy equipment was kept, so men and trucks were dispatched to claim theirs, including the appliances that had been shipped to the men back in Texas, where they were painted khaki and serial numbers mysteriously appeared on each. They were now part of the unit's equipment.

"While there, we saw a trailer with two large generators that seemed to be unclaimed, so we claimed it," Parrish says.

"We backed a truck up just like we owned it, and drove away," Parrish adds. There were no identifying numbers on the generators, but that didn't take long to remedy.

"We had all these refrigerators, and now we had the power to run them," Parrish continues, "so just about everyone had access to one.

"We had to keep the beer cold," he notes.

They were at Gia Lai for about three weeks, checking their equipment, testing firing their guns, then firing missions to support the paratroopers. Just about all of the men favored the new M-109 self-propelled howitzer mounted on a tracked vehicle, as opposed to the older howitzer that they had at the armory in Bardstown that had to be towed by a five-ton truck. When it came time to fire, the truck had to stop, and the howitzer had to be uncoupled, then positioned. When they needed artillery fire in a different direction, the men had to pick up the tail and turn it in the direction you wanted to fire. This took time. Not so with the new M-109. The gun turret was hydraulically operated and could rotate 360 degrees in a fraction of the time required to reposition a towed howitzer, which also took a lot of brute force. If you used high-angle fire, the tube on the M-109 elevated electrically, whereas with the towed howitzer, you had to crank the tube upward by hand. They were quickly learning the first order of the day in Vietnam—dig in. Wherever they went, they spent a lot of time filling sandbags, building bunkers, making their living quarters as comfortable as they could under wartime conditions. It didn't take long for them to form opinions about the war. They looked around and saw huge mountains of supplies and weapons, everything you would need to win a war, and wondered what six howitzers could do that hadn't already been done many times over.

"We're not meant to win this war," Jerry Janes recalls feeling. "We're just putting in time here.

"Once you realized the situation, then it became a matter of looking out for yourself, your friends, just making certain that you got home safely," Janes adds.

"It looked like the people didn't want to help themselves," Tom Raisor remembers. "I got the feeling they just wanted to be left alone to plant their rice.

"I really wasn't against the war, and really, I don't know when, at what point I changed my mind," he adds.

"I didn't get very close to the native people at all," Parrish says. "I know there's gotta be good people as well as bad people anyplace you go. But I couldn't tell one from the other, so I didn't trust any of 'em."

There were carpenters, electricians, builders, craftsmen of all sorts in the unit, so you could take a bad location and turn it into one that was reasonably comfortable. That's when they were told to get ready to move out, to head south on Highway 1 to an artillery location known as Hill 88.

They left on Thanksgiving Day, 1968, and relieved—one gun at a time—a regular army artillery unit that had been on 88 for three months. They left a lot of junk up there, so the first few days were spent cleaning up the area. The hill, eighty-eight meters above sea level, was an ideal position to defend. At the very top, a platoon of infantry was dug in to provide protection for the guns.

"It was the best position we had the whole time we were in Vietnam," Parrish says. "We had the top. We could see all around us.

"The guys on the top of the hill, the paratroopers, had just come out of the bush, out of the jungle, out of the swamps, so I guess for them, this duty was almost like going on rest and recuperation leave," Parrish continues. "They had hot food, clean clothes. They'd be with us for a month or so, then another group would rotate in."

"Once we found out that we were going to Hill 88, there was a certain amount of fear," Janes remembers, "but after we got out there, got sandbagged in, it was a damn good position, it was easy to defend." If you had to be on a hill, then 88 was probably one of the best you could find. There was no brush close by. No jungle. No place for the enemy to hide. And you held the high ground in all directions.

"I did not have the fear on Hill 88 that I had in other places we went," Janes says.

As the weeks slipped by, life on 88 began to take on a dull routine: work on your bunkers, keep the place clean, fire your missions, play a little basketball, drink a little beer. They played with the mule, too, a four-wheel, rear-drive, do-everything vehicle. And somewhere along the line, some of the men took a liking to a three-legged dog that wandered onto the hill and named it Gertrude. As days became weeks and the weeks became months, letters from loved ones became more important, taking on a significance every bit as great as it was for those receiving the letters they sent back home.

"Be careful, don't go out at night," Tom Raisor's mother counseled him in letter after letter because she had heard on the evening news that most of the fighting took place after dark.

There was sniper fire, too, usually when the men went on supply runs. "Some jerk would be up in the hills firing on a jeep or a truck down on the road, and we'd get a message, we'd start looking for him, we'd locate him, and we'd spend half a million dollars blowing that hillside away," Parrish relates. And there were the "hip-shoots"—when the battery would pack all its gear, leave the hill, and go into the jungle, the Au Shau Valley, the Roung-Roung Valley, and fire at targets they were told couldn't be hit from Hill 88. Then they returned to the hill.

"We were beginning to get the hang of wartime artillery by this time," Raisor says. "We were getting used to the weather, our shirtsleeves were cut off, our hats were pulled down, we were beginning to look like we'd been there awhile, and we were more at ease because nothing had happened."

There were three rows of concertina wire with razor edges around the perimeter. Two were side by side, and the third was placed on top. From the ground to the top of the wire was about seven feet. There were two-man guard bunkers back about 50 feet from the wire, and each bunker was about 150 feet from the next. Phu gas (jet fuel with a thickener, similar to napalm) poured into barrels was spotted around the perimeter and positioned so that when it was ignited, it would shoot out toward the enemy. They did their work well on Hill 88, and the unit was rated as one of the very best artillery outfits in Vietnam. Unfortunately, that brought a lot of high brass to the hilltop to watch them shoot, to see if Battery C was as good as everyone said.

Once, they took the guns down to the beach, a few miles away, so they could fire into the back of a mountain that they couldn't reach from Hill 88. For some reason, a general from a rear area showed up and wanted to direct the fire from a helicopter. All six guns were firing, and every time a round hit the side of the mountain, there was a secondary explosion, which meant they were hitting something such as ammunition or explosives. Then the general got them on the radio and told the battery commander: "We want you to fire one gun into the mountain and see what we get. I want it to fire six rounds."

"Well, they picked my gun, 'cause we were probably the fastest one of the bunch," said Charles M. Stone, who was chief of the Gun 4. Then the battery commander came over and said to Stone, "He wants you all to fire six rounds into the mountain."

"That's fine," Stone replied.

Boom! Boom! Boom! Boom! Boom! Boom! The ground shook from the six thunderous explosions in rapid sequence. Then the general landed and angrily shouted at the captain: "I told you I wanted one gun to fire! I didn't want all six guns firing!"

"Sir, only one gun was firing," the captain replied.

"Don't lie to me," the general hollered. "I know what's going on. You're firing one gun, then another, down the road like that. You're firing them all. No gun fires that fast."

The general was a bit calmer by now, and he told the captain that he wanted the same gun to fire six rounds again into the mountain, then he climbed aboard his copter and took off.

"Do you gentlemen think you all can fire any faster?" the captain asked Stone.

"Be no problem," Stone replied. So they pumped 'em out

faster than the first time. Then Stone looked up, saw the helicopter coming down about as fast as it could, watched it make a very bumpy landing, and smiled as the general got out and stalked angrily toward the captain.

"He tore that captain from one end to the other," Stone recalls.

"Sir, we only fired one gun," the captain replied, somewhat meekly.

"Don't tell me. Nobody can fire that fast. I've been in this man's army too long." By now, a small crowd of artillerymen was watching from a distance, and laughing.

"Well, I'll tell you what I'm gonna do," the general told the captain. "I'm gonna fly up behind this gun, and I want to see it." Then the general strode toward his helicopter, but not before taking a parting shot at the captain, saying, "I don't believe you."

"So the captain came over to our gun," Stone continues, "tears just about in his eyes, 'cause the general was rippin' him good, and says, 'Sergeant Stone, do you think you can pump 'em any faster?' "

"We can smoke it," Stone answered.

"We pumped 'em out; that general came right down, ran over to the captain and shook his hand," Stone adds.

"I'd never have believed it if I hadn't seen it," the general said to the captain. "Tell you what I'll do right now," the general said. "For each one of these men, I'll give you ten men."

"No. You can't have none of 'em," the captain replied.

There was another artillery location a few miles down that straight stretch of Highway 1 that was known as the "bowling alley." It was called Fire Base Tomahawk, and gradually the men were picking up on it. There was a battery of 105 howitzers over there. "We were in communication with everyone around us at all times, including the people on Tomahawk," Raisor says. "Everything in the world was going on over there. There was sniper fire all the time. There was incoming mortar fire."

"It was a bad hill," Parrish explains. "Bunkers collapsed. A guard post got washed down a hill in a storm. A guy was killed in a truck accident.

"I guess I finally came to the conclusion that it was a jinxed hill," he adds. "It had a terribly bad reputation."

Nevertheless, life went on atop Hill 88, although everyone kept an eye on Tomahawk, hoping that it wasn't in their future, hoping that it would go away.

But even on a good hill, such as 88, bad things can happen.

David Unseld and Reuben Simpson, close friends for years, were in a guard bunker on Hill 88. It had been raining heavily. It was one of the coldest and darkest nights.

"I'm gonna get some coffee," Unseld said.

"Will you bring me back a cup?" Simpson asked.

Unseld was gone but a couple of minutes. When he returned from the mess tent with the coffee, their guard bunker had disappeared completely. Unseld fired off a flare, looked down the steep hill, and saw a pile of sandbags, timber, wire, and an arm sticking up out of the rubble, waving a flashlight that was clenched tightly, the beam on to let rescuers know where the man was.

Unseld called for help, then scrambled down about 150 feet to where Simpson was tangled in razor-sharp wire, just a few inches from his face.

"Had I rolled another foot, I'd have no face," he remembers.

"There were claymores all over the hill, and I had the detonators and wires in my hand," he says. "I was afraid somebody coming down to help me might set something off."

Had he not been wearing his flak jacket, field jacket, and a poncho, he would have been cut to ribbons. The back of his left hand was badly cut and required several stitches; in the morning, he was taken to the hospital at Phu Bai.

And there were the unusual moments, too. "I got this call one day from a lieutenant who identifies his target as 'infantry in the open,'" Parrish remembers.

"Well, that was enough for us to fire," he adds.

"I want one gun to shoot and follow my instructions," the lieutenant said over the radio.

"We must have fired at least twenty-five rounds following this crazy path that led up a mountainside," Parrish says. "There was a forward observer out there and a helicopter overhead, giving us directions."

A short time later, Parrish heard on the radio: "End of mission. I'll get back to you later with a body count."

A few hours later, the unidentified lieutenant called Parrish from a different location on another channel and told him: "Hey, you guys shot a tiger for me."

"He was a taxidermist back home," Parrish remembers, "and he tanned the hide, mounted the head, and shipped it all home."

They also killed a panther, a deer, and two elephants coming out of a tunnel carrying supplies and a field piece for the North Vietnamese.

Nevertheless, Tomahawk was getting ever closer, inching inexorably toward Battery C. Twice, they packed their gear, took their howitzers, and went over there to fire missions that they were told could not be done from Hill 88. "I guess they were trying to break us in easy to the fact that we'd be moving to Tomahawk," Raisor explains. On one of the hipshoots there, they lost their battery commander, Capt. Lyle Thompson.

The weather was bad that day on Tomahawk. It was foggy. You could hardly see the end of the barrel on a gun. There was a forward observer out there, but he couldn't see anything. For some reason, Thompson decided that he would direct the fire from a helicopter. Stanley Stone, an enlisted member of the battery, was going to go along, but he didn't have his helmet at that moment. So someone else, a lieutenant who did have his helmet, climbed aboard with Thompson, and they took off, accompanied by a second helicopter, a gunship, for protection. A second gunship joined them when they were in the air. The target: suspected enemy positions a few miles away.

"I was talking to him as he was adjusting fire, the rounds hit, and I was waiting for him to tell me if we had hit the target," Raisor says.

"I waited and waited. There was no word. I thought the radio had gone dead, but there was a second radio he could use, but I didn't hear anything," Raisor adds. "I told the other two helicopters that we had lost contact with Thompson, and would they try and locate him." They searched the rest of the day, but couldn't spot him. Later that day, the men returned to Hill 88. Next morning, there were about eighty helicopters scouring the jungle. Four days later, they spotted the wreckage of Thompson's helicopter and a gunship that went along to provide protection, which had been shot down. The feeling of the men about their captain seemed to be this: "He was well liked by everyone, a good officer who knew his way through the army maze, but he should not have gone on this mission. It was someone else's job." A few weeks later, the battery's executive officer, Lt. Charles Harbin, was promoted to captain and became the unit's new commanding officer.

They continued their firing missions, their hipshoots, into the spring of 1969. "We'd go off the hill for a day or two, maybe a week and a half, but we'd always go back to Hill 88," Raisor says. At times, the jungle was so dense, the engineers would have to carve out a road for their big guns. They usually had earth-moving equipment with them to dig gun pits. They'd fire at night, move during the day, then fire again at night. This went on for some time.

Just before they were scheduled to return to Hill 88 from a three-week hipshoot in the Roung-Roung Valley, they found out that they would be going to Tomahawk to set up their own fire base.

Not much larger than some of the backyards in Bardstown, Tomahawk had been cut out of the side of a giant hill in the shape of a saddle, with three levels. It was very easy for the enemy to get there from above, a little more difficult to reach it from below. There was a railroad tunnel at the low end of the hill.

"No one was happy about this bit of bad news," Raisor says.

"It was a bad hill, and I didn't look forward to it," Janes remembers.

"It was scary," Charles Stone recalls.

"Moving to Tomahawk didn't sit too well with the men," Parrish adds. "We talked about it constantly. It never left our minds."

A few weeks earlier, the army began an infusion program with Battery C—slowly splitting the unit apart, taking some of the men and moving them to other units, and bringing in newcomers to replace them. The military reason for this was simple: to avoid a heavy reduction in personnel in one unit when the time came for the men to go home. Infusion provided for a slow, steady turnover of manpower. This was the primary reason for infusion. The program also helped to avoid a heavy loss in one unit from one community in the event that unit was overrun.

Teddy Marshall found out on Hill 88 that he would be leaving Charlie Battery soon and heading down south, to Chu Lai, to join a towed artillery unit.

"I didn't like it at first; I really felt bad about it. I felt that we were a better unit than most because we were able to work so well together," he says. "Now they were breaking us up.

"So I partied with the guys before I left, said my good-byes, and was gone," he adds.

"I could see very quickly that we took a turn down," Parrish says, "but a short time later, I could see we took a turn up, because a lot of the guys that came to us came from an unhappy environment and had now found a much happier environment with us." Parrish, a builder by trade, was put in charge of a twenty-man advance party and sent to Tomahawk to set up a fire base, to work on bunkers, set up a perimeter, try to make the place livable and workable so the battery could begin firing as soon as it moved in.

Tomahawk actually was a saddle about seventy-five feet above Highway 1. Everywhere you looked, you could see ground that was much higher, a situation that no one in the battery liked, but could do nothing about.

"We didn't like the enemy looking down our throats," Janes says.

On the high ground at the front end of the saddle was the ever-present platoon of 101st paratroopers. Just below and on somewhat level ground was an old bunker that other troops had used. It was a mess, and it took six days to make it halfway livable. Parrish and his work crew put their bunks on top of it and slept there because it was too hot to sleep inside. If you stood up and looked north, toward slightly higher ground, you'd see the 101st. Past the 101st was Highway 1, which made a couple of horseshoe bends and ran downhill. There were mountains all around. The men worked during the day in near-hundred-degree heat, and slept on the bunker at night. One night, though, a loud explosion roused them at one A.M. Then another, closer. They got off the roof and ran inside the bunker. Another explosion, closer than the last. There were six explosions, each closer than the last. "We could hear each round getting closer," Parrish says. "It was a mortar attack, and they were walking them in. The last round exploded just outside their bunker. But the paratroopers had spotted a muzzle blast and opened up with a .50-caliber machine gun on a spot on a mountainside just across Highway 1. Later, they also took some sniper fire, but it was from long range and didn't bother them.

"That was the first time I'd come under fire," Parrish says, "and I didn't like it one damn bit."

A few of the men then went up and talked to the paratroopers, who told them, "Go back to sleep and don't worry about it because it happens all the time."

Ten days later, the rest of the battery arrived, ninety officers and men, their ranks reduced because of the infusion program.

Three weeks in the Roung-Roung Valley and Elephant Valley had been hard on the men of Charlie Battery. The food left a lot to be desired. There was so much chlorine in the water, you couldn't drink it. That's why the men all had Kool-Aid sent from home. Milk was so bad, you didn't want to taste it. It was so hot when David Unseld drove Gun 3 up the hill to Tomahawk and parked it in the pit, the engine wouldn't start again.

"I was still in the gun when I was told to get my gear together and get on over to the helicopter pad, I was being transferred out," Unseld remembers.

"I was not happy about this, I was upset, I didn't want to leave my friends," he explains. "I grew up with Larry Johnson, Teddy Marshall, Bit Blanford.

"I got on the helicopter, went to Phu Bai, joined up with several others from Battery A and Battery B, and we flew to Quang Tri, a few miles south of the demilitarized zone and into another world," Unseld says.

"The first thing they did was ask me if I wanted to go to a firing battery or a service battery," he recalls, "and I remembered that service battery got everything, the firing battery got what was left.

"I wanted to stay back where they had the ice cream, hot food, clean clothes, so I said, 'I'll take the service battery.'

"Oh, my God, they fed you like a human," he remembers.

"If I had it to do over, I'd volunteer and do my two years," he adds. "There was not a lot of rank to be filled in the Guard. It was mostly who you knew, who you were related to."

About one-third of the men on Tomahawk were strangers. It took them a while to get the housekeeping routine down pat. They never stopped working on their bunkers. The perimeter drew a lot of their attention, too. The high hills around them were a constant reminder of the threat of attack. "We tried to stay as alert as possible, hoping that we'd beat the jinx, that nothing would happen to us," Parrish says. From time to time, the men would spot a glint of sun off a rifle, or a reflection off field glasses.

"When will they hit us?" Jerry Janes wondered from the first moment he arrived on that hill.

"Will they attack us tonight?" Raisor wondered.

"We all talked about how difficult it would be to defend the fire base if it were attacked," Parrish says. "I don't ever think we weren't thinking about that. It was constantly on our minds." Most of the men had the feeling they were constantly being watched. The jungle was so close to the barbed wire that enemy soldiers could walk to the edge of the brush and not be seen.

In early May, the battery commander, Captain Harbin, went home on emergency leave and was replaced by his executive officer, Tom Eatmon. A few days later, Eatmon brought in Lt. Dan Doyle to be his executive officer. Both had artillery backgrounds. Both were members of the Second Battalion, 138th Artillery. Both could see that a few bolts had to be tightened, that some of the priorities needed to be put back in their proper place.

"We needed to redesign a few things," Eatmon remembers.

"Charlie Battery was a good outfit, trained well, tightly knit, they knew what they were doing," he adds. "I can recall one time we had all six guns firing at the same time on separate missions."

A few weeks after they were there, the two officers challenged one of the gun crews to a shootout, to boost morale, to try and get to know the men better. Eatmon asked the gun sergeant to select a target. He picked a tree on a mountain way out. He got in his gun, sighted, fired, and missed the tree. Eatmon and Doyle got in and sighted. " 'Now, let 'er go,' " Eatmon recalls shouting. "We fired and missed the mountain. We went completely over the hill.

"I could hear laughter and carryin' on behind us; the men were really enjoyin' this," he remembers.

"But now we had a hundred-pound projectile zooming out there someplace, so I ran to the FDC [Fire Direction Center] and got them to figure out where it would hit," Eatmon says.

"Then Dan and I sweated it out for about four hours, but nothing happened, so I guess it landed in a rice paddy somewhere," he concludes.

Tomahawk had been taking sniper fire for several days, off and on. So Eatmon and Luther Chappel, the first sergeant, went up to talk to the airborne platoon leader, told him about the sniper, who so far hadn't come close to hitting anyone or anything, and that they believed enemy soldiers were probing the perimeter at night. Then Eatmon and Chappel continued to the top of the hill. They looked around and checked the wire. There were trip flares, claymore mines, barbed wire stretched out on the ground. But Eatmon wasn't pleased, and told Chappel: "If they ever come through here, we're in deep shit."

A few days later, they got a line on the sniper. An airborne lieutenant, over six feet tall, who drew fire every time he went anywhere on the hill, spotted movement on the hillside about six hundred yards away. He ran to the top of the hill, where the 101st had a .50-caliber machine gun on the roof of the bunker, shouting, "I got him spotted!" Eatmon and Doyle heard this, saw him running toward the machine gun, and ran after him, tackling him just before he got there. They held him on the ground and shouted, "Don't shoot him! They might get someone up there who can hit something!"

Despite the threat of attack, life did become routine—fire your missions, drink a little beer, watch movies, sleep. And when you weren't doing any of those, you filled sandbags. The six howitzers were spotted at various locations on the hill and put in gun pits, or "burms." A bulldozer would scrape out a hole in the ground, then earth would be piled up around it maybe four or five feet high. A pit would resemble a horseshoe. The howitzer was then driven into the burm and sandbagged. Close by, maybe fifty yards away, were the bunkers for the gun crews who were not on duty. They were well built. Some had heavy timbers and sandbags two and three high on the roof. They could, the men hoped, withstand a rocket-propelled grenade or a satchel charge.

Considering they were in a war zone, the men lived pretty well. They had their refrigerators, washing machines, ice makers. When there was nothing left but Carling Black Label, they'd make a beer run. Food was decent, but not great. They had a shower near the edge of the perimeter and close to the road that curled around the hill.

"I got off a shift at two o'clock one night and walked down to the shower with a flashlight and rifle and wasn't too concerned," Parrish says. "Then I saw this tarantula that blew me away. A dinner plate wouldn't cover it. I said, 'To hell with it,' and decided that I really didn't need a shower that night."

The key bunker on the hill was the Fire Direction Center. It was well built with sandbags and heavy timber and was surrounded by three rows of concertina wire. It was about forty-five feet long and divided into two sections, the working area and sleeping quarters. There were small portholes and a front entrance, but no door. Just inside, there was a wall of timber and sandbags a few feet from the opening to prevent anyone from firing directly into the bunker from the outside. To get inside, you would have to turn right or left.

"When we got a fire mission, the first thing we did was relay that information to Headquarters Battery," Raisor explains. "Now we both had the same information. We plotted the information on our maps and charts, such as elevation, range, wind, and they plotted the same information on their maps and charts, verifying our information and keeping us from making a mistake and possibly firing into our own troops. So everything we shot at, Headquarters Battery had to verify as the correct information that we were going to send to the guns."

It was extremely hot, and just as humid, on Wednesday, June 8, 1969, and the men were bored, restless. They hadn't done much for several days, except work on their bunkers and fire their missions. Friends were being transferred to other units. Strangers were taking their places and bringing with them drug problems and questionable work habits. If you're a company commander of another unit and you are told to transfer several men to another unit, you are going to get rid of the problem people and keep the good soldiers.

Eatmon, the battery commander, left that afternoon on leave for Hawaii to meet his wife. While morale wasn't too bad, it wasn't up where it should be. When you find yourself in a situation such as this, you forget to do the little things you normally would. You get careless. Then you begin to think. It was quiet yesterday. It was quiet last week. It will be quiet tonight. And they hadn't fired too many missions lately, nor had they heard any enemy gunfire.

"Why don't we see if we can snatch some food somewhere that everyone will like," Jodie Haydon suggested.

"Good idea," Guardsman Gary Bradbury said. "Why don't we have a cookout?"

"Yeah, it would be a great uplift for everyone," Haydon added.

They'd been on a steady diet of boiled beef lately, and they were sick of it. The battery had good cooks. They just didn't have too much to work with.

So Parrish took a three-quarter-ton truck and three or four men and headed for Phu Bai, because that's where the big food supply depot was. Better yet, he knew there were National Guard troops there, and they always took care of each other.

"Go in and see what you can do," the guard at the gate told the men from Battery C.

"We did pretty well," Parrish remembers. "We found two big cases of hamburger patties, some hot dogs, and all the buns you'd ever need, all destined for an officers' club."

Then they hit the beer depot and snatched a number of cases of various brands. "We just drove in, acted like we belonged there, and emptied a big refrigerator," Parrish says. "Since the refrigerator was now empty, shelves weren't needed, so we took them to use on the grill we were going to make." One of the men spotted a barrel, and they grabbed that, too.

"What the hell are they doing here?" one of the guards hollered at another, but by this time, they were on their way to the ice-making plant, where they filled two large coolers they had brought with them, tossed some more ice in the back of the truck, and were on their way back to Tomahawk before anyone realized what their mission was.

"The guys were thrilled, just tickled," Parrish says, "and the rest of the day, all they talked about was having a grand evening of hamburgers and all the cold beer you could drink."

They set up a grill, using a refrigerator shelf and half of the barrel, tossed in some charcoal they made, and the party was on by five P.M.

"We had hamburgers and beer for about 150 men, including the 101st," Parrish said. "We didn't have parties very often, but when we did, we sure did it up right." When it began to get dark, they set up their movie screen in the maintenance tent and watched a James Bond movie, *You Only Live Twice*. But before it was over, it began to rain so hard that they couldn't hear the soundtrack—a perfect situation for North Vietnamese troops to position themselves just outside the perimeter.

When the rain ended, the men returned to the guns, their bunkers. They played cards, wrote letters home, caught a little sleep.

"Everyone had a ball. It helped morale, which wasn't all that bad, it was a real good pick-me-up, and was much appreciated by everyone," Parrish says of the barbecue.

"But it was the calm before the storm, as things turned out," he adds.

When the rain stopped, the temperature dropped sharply and there actually was a chill in the air, so the cooks left a large pot of chicken noodle soup out. "It'll stay warm awhile, and the men can come up from the guard bunkers and the guns and get warm," one of them said.

The night of the attack, Doyle was in the command bunker where he and Eatmon slept. Around eleven P.M., the first sergeant, Chappel, came in and asked Doyle if he could bunk with him that night because the downpour earlier that evening had flooded his quarters.

"Sure, bring your gear and come on in," he told Chappel.

"It was a very active battery, they fired a lot of missions," Doyle said. "I was impressed with the men, they were extremely close-knit." Doyle and Chappel, who hadn't been with the battery very long, either, talked for a while, then went to sleep. It was very hot inside, so they slept in their shorts.

"Two explosions got us out of bed and awake in a hurry," Doyle says. "I knew it was incoming rather than outgoing, so I looked out one of the slits in the wall and didn't see the results of the explosions.

"I told Luther to go to the perimeter and check on security, then report back to me," Doyle recalls. "I never saw Chappel again." The first sergeant was killed about thirty-five or forty feet from the bunker, probably the first person to die that night. Doyle left Eatmon's bunker and ran to the executive officer's post close by, where there was communication to the guns, and asked Buck Harned, the chief of smoke, who was in charge of the physical operation of the guns—ammunition inventory, making certain the guns were working—what was going on.

"My assessment at that time was that they were not inside, that we were taking mortar rounds to soften us up for an attack," Doyle explains. "Had I thought for a moment they were inside the perimeter, I never would have sent Luther out there." Now they had to identify the direction of the incoming, then select the counter mortar plan that they would implement to send the ninety-eight-pound projectiles crashing into the barren areas where they thought the mortars might be set up. But it was too late.

"I think they're already inside," Harned told Doyle.

"Are you sure?"

"I think those explosions are RPGs [Rocket Propelled Grenades]," Harned answered.

"Okay, let's get on the land lines to the guns and get the men out of them," Doyle said to the radio operator, a youngster of perhaps twenty who was very new in the battery. But he couldn't contact anyone. And the men on the six guns were already buttoned up firing counter mortar fire. They were trained to do this—to react to incoming. They didn't have to be told.

"I reached for one of the phones, but then I heard Buck shout, 'Incoming!'

"I saw a big flash of bright light, and then I heard a deafening explosion, and I was thrown from the front of the bunker to the back, a distance of about six feet. And then I didn't remember anything for about twenty seconds." Harned took shrapnel in the stomach. The radio operator was hit in the upper left arm; it was a clean wound—through and through—but he began to scream. Doyle wasn't sure if he was hit, but both legs were beginning to lose their feeling, becoming numb.

Two or three minutes later, another RPG blew through the room, there was another blinding flash, the same deafening explosion, and Doyle flew across the room again, and lay there, at the base of the wall, shaken and groggy.

"Everybody all right?" he shouted.

"Yeah!"

By this time, the hill seemed to be exploding.

"I thought about leaving the bunker then, but my main concern was getting the men out of the guns," he says. The first RPG had torn all the wires out, so there was no communication with anyone now. The guns were laid out in a "lazy W" pattern, which was normal gun placement.

"Buck and I went to the door and started yelling for Gun 4 to see if we could establish voice contact, and if we could, to tell them to get on the land line to the other guns and tell the men to get out of them," Doyle says. As soon as they started yelling, a third RPG went off just outside the front door and hit a jeep, partially destroying it, but not hurting anyone.

"Let's get to the FDC!" Doyle shouted, and the three of them ran out the door and down the hill about thirty yards. When they got close, Doyle shouted, "We're coming in! Don't shoot!" His legs hurt something awful, but the three made it inside. His legs were bleeding badly—ripped apart by metal. So was one arm.

"As soon as I got inside, I think I started going into shock," he says. "I became very lightheaded and very cold. In fact, I was freezing." He was taken to the far end of the FDC and placed on the ground. "From then on, things became very foggy," he remembers. "I heard people talking on the radio, yellin' orders, and that's all."

Lt. Jim Lee, an FDC officer with Battery B at Phu Bai, who

had been called up a week earlier to help out in the FDC at Battery C, remembers, "The initial attack killed Chappel and wounded Doyle, so we lost our leadership in the first five minutes.

"Doyle was wounded and under a table and said to me, 'You're in command,' " Lee adds.

The young radio operator was panic-stricken, screaming, hollering for his mother. They couldn't get him to calm down and stop.

"Doyle, using his good arm, knocked him cold," Parrish says.

The Fire Direction Center relied on big truck batteries that they continually charged to run their radios. To do this, they had to go outside the bunker and several yards away, and start the generators. Normally, someone else did this, but on this particular night, Tom Raisor told the rest of his crew, "I'll go out and start the generators, I need to stretch my legs for a few minutes." The guns had just finished firing their scheduled missions for the night. The crews were either taking it easy in the gun pits, talking or loading projectiles in the guns on the left side, powder on the right, just in case they were unexpectedly called on for fire support. David Collins and two others were on their way to the mess tent for some of that warm chicken soup and to take it easy for a few minutes.

"I had already wrapped the rope around the pulley on the generator and was getting ready to pull it when I heard this god-awful explosion, looked up, and saw the mess hall flying through the air, tin and wood going in all directions." Raisor ran back into the FDC, started shaking people awake, then got on the radio to battalion.

"I thought it was incoming, but you still wake everybody up just in case there's a ground attack," he says. In a few minutes, the entire hill was exploding.

Lt. Thomas R. Ice, the fire direction officer for the battalion back at Gia Lai, was talking to Raisor.

"We're taking incoming," Raisor told Ice, then the radio went dead. It came back on a few minutes later, and Ice told Raisor to "implement the counter mortar plan," which meant that each of the six guns would fire into predetermined locations, where the incoming fire most likely would be coming from. Communication was lost again, and for the next two hours, it was on and off, mostly off. But the gun crews didn't have to be told what to do. They were already firing counter mortar rounds into the mountains and beyond. Just before the mess hall blew, a perimeter guard reported seeing a flare go off above the jungle. Then all hell broke loose. It was thunder and lightning. Rocket-propelled grenades—fired from one-man–operated rockets with a large explosive charge in the warhead capable of penetrating ten inches of armor—began exploding everywhere. Then they heard an explosion that was new to them—satchel charges, small bags of TNT about two inches by three and a half inches and weighing a half pound with five-second timers. The men inside the FDC were firing through small portholes at shapes running by. It was very dark.

"Some of us had our clothes off, some had their shoes off, others had their shoes on, and some had their helmets on and not much of anything else, but we all had our flak jackets on," Parrish says.

"Try as I might, I really couldn't see anything at first," he recalls. "But after the explosions lighted up the area, we could see shapes running all over the place, maybe five to ten feet away, but they never got in really tight because of the wire."

There were explosions everywhere. Satchel charges were exploding on the roof, but there were plenty of sandbags up there, so no hot metal came through. Parrish, Raisor, Jodie Haydon, and James Ice were among those in the FDC at this time. All were either on the radios or firing out the small windows. They could see the North Vietnamese running toward the guns. They could hear the explosions behind and above them on the hill, up where the airborne platoon, the exec post, and the communications bunker were located. From the inside, it sounded as if the communications bunker was taking a beating.

Larry Johnson was in charge of communications for the firing battery. Wires ran from each of the six big guns, all the perimeter bunkers, the mess hall, the exec post, and the Fire Direction Center—the heart and soul of the battery. About eighteen wires, most of them underground, ran to a spot just outside the right entryway to the communications bunker. There they were attached to a stake, more like a fence post, driven into the ground. If there was a problem with a line, Johnson could step outside a few feet, put a phone on the wire, and get a good idea where the trouble might be.

Johnson's bunker was on the high part of the saddle, about thirty yards below the airborne platoon, one of the first areas hit by the North Vietnamese that night. The communications bunker, or wire bunker, as everyone called it, was twelve feet wide by twenty-four feet long, and it was built to last. But no one there ever thought that it would take such a ferocious assault, absorb so many satchel charges and RPGs, have so much enemy fire directed toward it. The back was built into the side of a small hill. Even so, there were heavy timbers, sandbags, and layers of sheet metal back there. You could walk off the top of that small hill and onto the roof, which was built with large twelve-by-twelve-inch beams, layers of steel sheet metal, and sandbags stacked three high on top of that. There were two entrances, one on the right, the other on the left. But you couldn't run or fire straight into the bunker, because a few feet inside the two openings there were walls of sandbags, timbers, and sheet metal. To get inside, you would have to turn either right or left.

"We were in our bunks just getting ready to go to sleep. Ronnie Simpson [who had been in the field with the 101st Airborne as a forward observer] was in his bunk. Ronnie McIlvoy [a radio operator and wireman] was sitting below on his bunk. There were no lights on, and we didn't expect any trouble at all that night," Johnson remembers.

"I think that first blast was a signal, then the North Vietnamese all opened up at once," he adds. "By this time, they were well inside the perimeter.

"They must have seen the wire that was concentrated outside my bunker on the right and mistaken us for the Fire Direction Center, so they concentrated on destroying us," Johnson continues. "I guess it was a blessing in disguise, though, because the FDC was the brains of the operation, and the battery would have been a real mess if they had destroyed it."

Four, maybe five satchel charges were tossed inside—first from the entrance on the left, then from the entrance on the right. The North Vietnamese alternated, left, right, left, right, until everything inside was destroyed. "It was like you were in a room full of BBs flying around," Johnson says. "Our equipment was destroyed, our weapons were destroyed, that beautiful floor that Ronnie Simpson had built became splinters of wood flying through the air." Johnson was on the floor in the left rear corner. Ronnie McIlvoy, who had been in his bunk against the left wall, was on the floor close to Johnson. Simpson, who had the bunk above McIlvoy's, was still up there. There was simply too much hot metal, too many bits of equipment and pieces of timber flying through the air. Some of the metal tore into Johnson's left ankle. The roof began to shake as five or six satchel charges exploded on top. Then it began to buckle. Simpson got out of his bunk, and he, Johnson, and McIlvoy huddled in the left rear corner of the bunker, which seemed the safest place to be. Satchel charges began to hit the front wall, then RPGs, and it began to crumble. In a few minutes, you could see the fires burning on the lower part of the hill. They couldn't get out on the right because North Vietnamese were on the level above them hurling satchel charges.

The airborne outpost on the top of the hill above them had been destroyed, and casualties were heavy. Now the North Vietnamese were attacking the exec post and the FDC. The communications bunker was almost gone. Nevertheless, it was still taking satchel charges and RPGs. There had been several other men in the bunker, but they had gotten out.

"What are we gonna do?" McIlvoy shouted over the explosions.

"We gotta get out of here!" Johnson hollered back. "We gotta go out the left side."

Simpson got up, ran to the left and out, headed toward the exec post and the Fire Direction Center, and was shot in the head as he sought cover by the exec bunker. His body was found close to the exec post.

The roof of the bunker was falling around them, so Johnson and McIlvoy ran out the left and hit the ground, Johnson in a small indentation in the earth about three inches deep, McIlvoy a few inches to Johnson's left on flat ground, his body more exposed. The bunker was now destroyed and burning, the wires had long since been blown away, yet they were still taking hits by RPGs and satchel charges.

Johnson could feel bits of hot metal hit his skin. If he was getting hit, then McIlvoy must be taking more shrapnel, because he was more exposed to the enemy. The North Vietnamese were still on the level above them and to their left. They probably couldn't see Johnson because he was tight against the bunker's wall. It's possible they could see McIlvoy. Regardless, they kept hurling satchel charges in their direction. Every one that exploded lifted them off the ground about two inches, then slammed them back to earth.

"I knew at this point I was dead," Johnson remembers. "We had no weapons. Eventually, they'd get us. I accepted it right on the spot." Satchel charges kept exploding close to them, lifting them off the ground.

"I told myself I'd welcome the next satchel charge, I'd welcome a hit and get it over [with]," Johnson says. "I was tired of being blown off the ground." But there was no letup. "I looked around, saw Ronnie, face pressed into the ground as hard as could be," Johnson remembers. "Another satchel charge hit just about on top of us, I looked around again, and Ronnie was gone."

Finally, gunfire from across the hill drove the North Vietnamese away from the bunker, the exec post, and the FDC. "I wasn't too well together, but I heard someone shout, 'Put the fire out!' So I got a bucket off the top of a fire barrel and started throwing water on the blazing bunker." That didn't work. So he ran, stumbled, crawled to the FDC and got inside, where he got a weapon and went to the entrance with Jodie Haydon, and they fired at shapes running around in front of them, out where the guns were.

Johnson was going into shock, so someone threw a blanket around him. At first light, he stood up and looked around the hill. He remembers seeing the flag flying at the top—shot full of holes, but still flying—and thinking of old war movies.

"You'd better go on up to the mess hall and get some water and wash off," Haydon told him. He was a mess. Clothes in tatters. No shoes. Ankle bleeding, covered with dirt. Roger Coffey, the medic, took one look at him and told him to get on up to the top of the hill and get aboard the helicopter that was taking wounded back to the hospital at Phu Bai.

"I think the North Vietnamese began to go through our perimeter wire during that really heavy rain," Parrish says. "If you couldn't hear the soundtrack of a movie and you were in the tent with it, how could you hear enemy troops slipping through wire?" If you went out one end of the FDC, there was a drop of about 150 feet to Highway 1. Out the other end, there were steps leading to bunkers above.

"Buck Harned was in the bunker above me and, although wounded, made it out and was helped down the hill and into my bunker," Parrish says. "He was bleeding, so I put him in a bunk and tried to find out what had happened up there.

"I knew it wasn't good, but I just didn't know how bad it was," Parrish recalls.

"Buck! What's happening up there?" He couldn't answer; he was hurt too badly.

"Basically, what I knew was that the enemy was runnin' all over the place at will," Parrish adds. Then he turned and shouted at Raisor: "We need gunships! Tell 'em we need the gunships! And we need copters to get the wounded out."

"This is going to kill the folks back home," Haydon said to Parrish as they continued firing at the running shapes outside.

David Collins and two others—so new in the battery, no one can remember their names—were just entering the mess hall. Unless something came up, they had fired their last mission for the night. It was about a hundred feet between the mess hall and Gun 4. The gun chief, Charles Stone, told Collins he would shout if they were needed.

A few minutes later, Stone heard the explosion as the mess hall blew up. Then he saw Collins and the other two men running up the slight hill toward the gun, shouting, "Gooks in the mess hall! Gooks in the mess hall!" Not far behind them, Stone saw a North Vietnamese running with a satchel charge that he threw into bags of gunpowder stacked close to Gun 4, and the powder went off.

By this time, there were about seventy North Vietnamese soldiers inside the perimeter, heavily armed with rocket-propelled grenades, satchel charges, and AK-47s, and wearing little or no clothing. They had cut through the wire in three locations. With their clothing off, they could tell quickly when their skin touched the barbs. Then they'd stop, slide to one side so as not to rattle the wire, and continue crawling. Before first light, between 150 and 180 enemy soldiers were inside the wire. Another 150 were believed waiting just outside, on the edge of the jungle, for the signal to join the assault.

Stone and two other men who had been in the gun crew only a day got in the gun and buttoned it up. " 'We don't have any fuses,' " Stone remembers saying. So one of the men climbed out, went somewhere, returned in a couple of minutes with fuses, pounded on the gun's door, and got back in. "I always told the men that if we ever came under ground attack, be sure some of you get in the burm so you can keep the enemy off the gun." That's where Collins and the two men with him went. But it became too hot to stay there. Gunpowder was exploding around them. "I told them to get to the bunker at Gun 6 and make sure that no one gets on top of our gun," Stone says.

"David went over into the other bunker and told me, 'Everything's fine. I'm watching the gun, everything's fine.' That's the last I heard from him. I was told that an RPG came through the back of the bunker, and shrapnel hit him in the back of the head."

Then Stone tried to back the gun out of the burm, to get it away from the intense heat, but he couldn't. It was dug in so well that it wouldn't move either forward or backward when they fired their missions. They fired some illumination rounds, which turn night into day for about two minutes, but no one in the gun could see anything. Stone could hear RPGs and satchel charges exploding everywhere. At times, the gun shook because there were so many explosions so close. Then an RPG hit a weld in the barrel where it joins the turret, and lodged there. The tube couldn't move either up or down, and the RPG was slowly burning its way toward the inside; when it did, it exploded. Stone got hit in an arm with shrapnel. A second man got hit worse. A third man was not hit. Then the powder ignited.

"Get the back door open, and let's get outta here!" Stone shouted.

"It won't open. It's stuck!"

Stone threw his body against it, the door opened, and he fell out on the ground. "I looked up, and there was nothing but fire and explosions everywhere," Stone remembers. Then the other two men tumbled out.

The situation at the Fire Direction Center was still pretty tense. North Vietnamese were swarming over the upper levels of the hill. Now another problem was developing: the twelve-volt batteries that powered the radios had to be recharged because communication was becoming less than dependable. This meant that someone would have to go outside to the generators, a few yards from the front entrance but inside the wire that circled the FDC, and start them. So Parrish, wearing his flak jacket and helmet, and carrying his rifle, went out while the men covered him from the windows and got them started on the first pull.

Stone, on his feet now at Gun 4, took a quick look toward the perimeter, where his brother, Stanley, was in a guard bunker. "The whole area was in flames," he remembers, "and I thought he was dead." Charles Stone and the two men with him were in the middle of a battlefield and not sure where to go or what to do, when he heard shouting coming from the direction of Gun 2, and recognized David Bishop's voice.

"Guys, our gun's on fire over here, so we're gonna come over," Stone shouted. "So don't you all do any shooting!"

"Come on over, we'll be watching for you."

Stone told the two men with him to watch and, as soon as he got over there, to follow him. But as soon as he took off, someone opened up with a machine gun, and he hit the ground, bullets kicking up the dirt around him.

"Stop shootin' at me!" Stone hollered. Then he got up and started running again, the machine gun opened up again, and he hit the dirt again.

"C'mon over," a voice hollered from Gun 2. "I don't hear nothin'." Stone got up again, but as soon as he did, the machine gun opened up again, and he was back in the dirt.

Then Stone heard a voice he recognized.

"Skip, everything's all right now! Go on over!" Spider Roberts shouted at Stone, who was called Skippy.

"Spider was talkin' to one of the regular army guys," Stone remembers, "and he had a gun to his head and said, 'You pull the trigger again, you're dead! That's our man!' " Stone got up and ran to the bunker near Gun 2, then motioned for the two other men to come over. He bandaged the wounds of the man who had been hit pretty bad by shrapnel. Then he looked toward the upper part of the hill and the Fire Direction Center and saw someone moving around an area where the generators were. "I had the rifle up on him, and I was ready to pull the trigger when he rose up, and I could see he had a helmet on," Stone adds.

"I still don't know who he was to this day, but he was almost a goner," Stone says.

Louis T. (Bit) Blanford was dog tired. He hadn't had much sleep for about a week. He'd been in the Roung-Roung Valley on a hipshoot. He'd pulled guard duty for the past three days. This particular day, he had worked in the mess hall, peeling potatoes, washing the dishes. They didn't let the Vietnamese work in the mess area. They wanted to keep them out of the area as much as possible, so this meant that the men in the battery took turns at KP. That night, he was scheduled to pull guard duty on the perimeter. But the gun sergeant realized that he probably couldn't stay awake, so Blanford traded duty with one of the men new in the unit.

"I didn't like the hill. It was set down real low, with mountains all around it," he remembers. "There was a railroad tunnel under the low end of the hill, and what we didn't know at the time was that the North Vietnamese were in there waiting for dark to hit us. They had blown the tracks far to the right and far to the left, so no trains could run through it."

Blanford did a little of just about everything on Gun 6. He was the driver, the ammunition carrier, the outside guy, which meant that it was his responsibility to keep the enemy off the gun, should they get into a tight situation. He could also fire the gun.

But that night, June 19, was one of the quietest he could remember in a long time. At one A.M., his gun fired three rounds toward what they suspected were supply trails in the mountains, something they did every night about the same time. Life had become routine on Tomahawk.

There was an ammunition hopper close to the gun, well sandbagged. Blanford crawled on top, took his shoes off, and stretched out on the top layer of sandbags. No matter it was misty, drizzling, dark as pitch. He was tired.

Then all hell broke loose. Screaming, hollering, explosions brought him back to reality.

"At first, I didn't know what was happening, nobody knew what was happening, so I jumped in the gun and fired illumination straight up," he remembers. Then he jumped out of the gun and saw that the top of the hill was in flames, there were explosions everywhere. Gun 6 had a .50-caliber machine gun mounted on top, and someone was up there firing it at the top of the hill. Whoever was on top jumped down and got in the gun, and he and another member of the gun crew fired more illumination. From time to time, Blanford handed them more illumination rounds.

RPGs and satchel charges were exploding everywhere, and the sky was full of tracers, all coming down from the top of the hill, he said.

"I could see one guy in particular standing on what appeared to be the roof of the airborne bunker, firing shoulder rockets, and I remember the red balls of fire coming down from the top," Blanford adds. "Every time I looked up there, I could see this one guy firing these red balls of fire."

There was an ammunition bunker close by with a .30-caliber machine gun on top, so Blanford ran over to the gun, aimed it toward the top of the hill, and fired, hoping to get that one North Vietnamese who was causing so much trouble, who appeared to be untouchable.

"I don't know if I hit him," Blanford says, "but I sure did get their attention, because they started to bang hell out of our gun, the ammo bunker.

"RPGs were going off everywhere, in front of me, on the right, the left, but most of 'em hit a big chain-link fence, about eight feet tall, that went about three-quarters of the way around the gun," Blanford says.

"I remember clearly the rocket that hit the fence, bounced off, exploded, and the small bits of metal that hit my back," he continues. "That fence took a lot of hits that night. Good God Almighty, I can still see the fence vibratin'.

"I remember thinkin' to myself, 'I'm scheduled to leave this unit in three days, so what the hell is goin' on here?'

"They never did hit the gun," he adds.

By this time, he was drawing so much fire, he knew he had to get out of there, so he ducked behind a fifty-five-gallon water barrel a few yards away and began firing his rifle at shapes on top of the hill.

"By now, they were poundin' hell out of the bunker, the gun, everything; I was out in the open. They were firin' at me, I knew I had to get out of there," he says. "That fifty-five-gallon water drum wasn't given' me much protection 'cause it was empty.

"I kept waitin' for the gunships to show up, but it seems like it was an hour and a half, at least, before I heard a helicopter," he remembers.

The gun sergeant and another man were inside, firing illumination. Blanford tossed a few more rounds in, just happened to look down the side of a hill close to where the gun was positioned, and saw twelve or thirteen North Vietnamese starting to climb up toward the gun. There were seven M-16s in the gun pit, loaded, with extra clips on the ground. He grabbed two rifles, ran about forty feet to a small trailer that belonged to the mess hall, and began firing down at the North Vietnamese. He emptied one clip, and the gun jammed. He fired the other, and it jammed, too, before the clip was empty, but he hit some of them, because they didn't continue up the side of the hill. He turned and took one step away from the trailer he was hiding behind. Then an RPG hit the other side and blew it up, and Blanford was covered with eggs and milk.

He was halfway to the gun pit, which was about forty feet distant, when he glanced toward the top of the hill.

"That same gook was up there on top of the roof, tryin' to get me. Then I saw three or four big red balls of fire comin' in my direction, but they all went behind me and hit the mess hall area," he remembers.

"Then I headed for our bunker, which was close by, but that guy on the hill knew where I was going, and he led me, he fired another red ball of fire at the bunker," Blanford explains. "I could see it comin', so I leaped toward the entrance, the rocket exploded just above the entrance, I got hit in both legs and a shoulder, knocked two guys aside in the doorway, and landed on the floor of the bunker."

He didn't know he had been hit at first. Then he felt his legs turn cold, reached down, felt the blood, and shouted at the two men firing out the entrance, "You son of a bitch, you shot me!" He didn't know until much later at the hospital, when they took the metal out of his legs, that he'd been hit with RPG fragments.

As soon as he landed on the floor of the bunker, an RPG came through, exploded, and knocked one man unconscious for a few minutes. The bunker withstood the attack pretty well. The four layers of sandbags around the walls and on the roof absorbed the RPGs and satchel charges. Another RPG did get through and exploded, and shrapnel hit David Collins in the head. Blanford had a flashlight, turned it on to see what damage had been done, and saw Collins on the ground by the entrance, dead.

He could hear the gunships overhead now. It was just about light. Blanford was standing by the door when he saw a green flare go off overhead. "I was told later they wanted to send in more troops, but somebody shot up the wrong-colored flare, and they withdrew," Blanford says.

At first light, word was passed from bunker to bunker: get the wounded up to the helicopter pad. Two men helped Blanford up there, and he was flown to the hospital at Phu Bai. "I remember seeing Jim Moore on the helicopter," Blanford says. "He was talkin' normal, but I guess he didn't know how bad hurt he was."

Blanford was in various military hospitals for about ten weeks. He returned to Kentucky August 31, 1969.

"I guess the good Lord was with me that night," he adds, " 'cause the guy I traded jobs with was killed in his guard bunker."

It was chaos, confusion, turmoil in the FDC at this time.

"One satchel charge came through the entrance, went off in the hallway, and knocked a half dozen people to the ground. Several other explosions shook the bunker," Raisor says. Men from other bunkers and guns, bleeding, burned, made their way to the FDC because it was still standing. Raisor suffered a concussion from the blast of the satchel charge, but he continued on the radios. "It felt like a dinner bell was ringing in my ear," he relates. Only the critically wounded were down. Everyone else fought back.

"We got one heavy blast on top that broke a twelve-by-twelve-inch beam, dropped the lights, and almost brought the roof down on us," Raisor says.

Raisor was on the radio: "We need gunships! We need support!"

"But they didn't want to come in because there was too much gunfire on the hill," he remembers. Finally, one gunship showed up.

"I need to know something about the hill so we'll know who we'll be shooting," the pilot told Raisor.

"Can you see the bunkers, the explosions?" Raisor asked.

"Yes!"

"The men are mostly in the bunkers, the people running around are the North Vietnamese," Raisor explained.

"Then he came right down, firing his rockets," Raisor recalls.

"I could hear the helicopter, he was shooting the hell out of the perimeter," Raisor adds.

Jerry Janes was in the pit, about twelve feet behind Gun 1. So were Ronnie Hibbs and Rich Daley. Bill Kinder, who was also in the crew, had stepped away for a few minutes. Kinder and Daley had just transferred into the unit. The men had finished their firing missions for the night and were loading gunpowder in the gun and seven or eight projectiles. Next, they put in three illumination rounds. Then they heard the first explosion that tore apart the mess hall at the other end of the hill. Janes thought it was incoming mortars and got ready to go back inside the gun.

Janes remembers that the explosions were pretty rapid as he headed for the rear door. Hibbs, who was inside the gun, looked out when he heard the explosions, and saw several fires. "I thought it was incoming," Hibbs says. "I didn't have no idea there was anybody within a mile of where we were." They were just about to close the door when Kinder came back, bleeding and burned, got into the gun, and collapsed on the floor in the rear, in great pain. Janes took a quick look, saw the hill on fire, buttoned up the door, and shouted,

"Hey! This is for real!" They fired into their designated areas, then they fired the three illumination rounds. The side hatch on the turret was still open, so Janes stuck his arm out to pull it shut. He could hear the buzz of shrapnel. Wood and dirt flew through the air. He took a quick look outside and saw three or four people in front of the gun. Two were already on top, trying to find a place where they could drop a satchel charge. Then the gun began to draw fire. Two satchel charges went off near the tracks, and the gun rocked. Two RPGs hit the side, then two landed on top. He took one more quick look, saw Gun 3, Jim Moore's gun, and it was a ball of fire. Then he buttoned up the hatch.

"We're in big trouble! We gotta get outta here!" Janes hollered.

Hibbs, who was by the back door, kicked it open and jumped out, and began to run toward their bunker, about forty feet away. A satchel charge went off just about under him, and he did two complete turns, landed on his feet, and kept on running toward the bunker, his clothes on fire. Just as Hibbs got out of the gun, an RPG penetrated and touched off the powder. Kinder and Daley were badly burned. Janes was hit in the arm and back, and his shirt was on fire. They got out and ran toward the bunker, too. Kinder stumbled and was barely moving, so Janes grabbed an arm and began to drag him. As soon as Hibbs reached the bunker, Bobby Stumph threw a blanket around him and got the fire out. Then he reached out and helped pull Kinder inside. The bunker was a mess. A satchel charge had landed under the table on which they played cards, and only splinters were left.

Stumph had one boot on and was about to pull the other on when the satchel charge was tossed inside, exploded, blew the boot away, tore the canvas top away from the sole, badly injured a foot, and blew a hole in the sheet-metal floor. Wood splinters from the table ripped his face and chin, and he was momentarily blinded. "I don't know how long it was before my sight returned," he says.

"My shirt was on fire when I ran into our bunker," Hibbs recalls. "Everything was blown up in there, but Bobby threw a blanket on me and got the fire out, then handed me a rifle.

"The guy who threw the satchel charge was still out there,

behind some rocks," continues Hibbs, who had his rifle pointed toward the rocks. Another man had crawled outside to an ammo dump and brought back a lot of hand grenades. He kept throwing them until one landed among the rocks and killed the North Vietnamese.

Then a C-47 began to circle, dropping flares, and the men could see, and the odds changed in their favor. "Once we could see them, we could hold our own," Hibbs explains.

"During the first fifteen or twenty minutes, I didn't think we were gonna make it," he adds.

Joseph Keeling, who worked in the maintenance section, was asleep in his bunker. The commotion outside woke him up. Then a satchel charge landed inside and went off, badly injuring the leg of one man by the door. Then another came in and slid across the floor and stopped under Keeling's bunk. "I didn't know what a satchel charge was, but I did hear this thump, thump, thump, so I got away from there, and it went off and blew my bunk apart and bent my M-16 so that I couldn't use it," he says. "It was dark, you couldn't tell who was hit, but we knew one person was hit because we could hear him screaming." Jack Lewis, maintenance section, was guarding the door so no one could get close enough to toss in another satchel charge. There wasn't much left of the maintenance area. The tent was shredded. The petroleum and lubricants bunker was blown up. "I guess they thought it was a guard bunker," Keeling says. The "mule," the four-wheel-drive vehicle that they all had so much fun with, was now just a steering column.

Wayne Collins, David's brother, was inside Gun 5, firing illumination. "I was standing up when all of a sudden it just lit up like daylight, almost blinding me, and I was knocked to the floor." Shrapnel ripped apart a leg, and he was bleeding badly from the upper thigh to the ankle. He was taken out of the gun and placed on a bunk while the fighting raged. His gun, better concealed than the others, was the last one firing when the RPG burned its way through on the left side and exploded. Another man inside was hit in the foot. Later, when the gunfire had slowed, Collins was taken to the FDC, and from there to a helicopter at first light. Though badly wounded, he never lost consciousness, and at one point asked one of the men carrying him, "Have you seen David?"

"I think he's all right," Stanley Stone said. But Wayne felt otherwise.

"If David was all right, then he'd have been there with me," Wayne says.

Reuben Simpson had just taken his boots off and was getting ready to go to sleep when he heard the explosion that destroyed the mess hall. He grabbed his M-16 and extra clips, which he always kept at arm's reach, got his .45 and an M-79 grenade launcher, and went to the entrance at the far end of the bunker. There was another entrance at the other end of the bunker, and somebody was there, too. An RPG missed the bunker, landed two feet outside one of the doorways, exploded, and blew a large beam that was part of the wall twelve feet across the bunker and into the rear wall. One of the men inside was lifted off the floor and slammed against the wall, too.

Jim Moore, who ran the day shift, had been in and out of the bunker that night.

"Jim was the first one to get in the gun," Tom Raisor remembers. "When he ran out of the bunker, he had on his boots, shorts, and an old T-shirt."

"Jim was able to fire illumination as the sappers ran around the hill, and he maintained his firing until we got illumination from other sources," Lieutenant Lee remembers.

"An RPG powered its way through the side of his gun, exploded inside, touched off the gunpowder, and blew the back door off the gun," Raisor explains. One man ran outside, on fire, and fell to the ground about twelve feet from the gun. Moore came out next, his clothes burned away. A third man was dead inside the gun.

"Jim didn't even have to come out of the bunker," a saddened Charles Stone remembers. Stone's Gun 4 was about a hundred yards from Moore's Gun 3.

Reuben Simpson was still firing out one end of the bunker toward a pile of rocks about sixty feet away, where enemy troops were crawling, but they never got close to the bunker.

"Seems like we fought for hours and hours," Simpson says, "but it really wasn't that long. When I went out at first light, I was amazed at what little was left. The whole hill was just about gone."

Later that morning, when he walked around the hill, one of

the bodies he saw was that of a North Vietnamese who'd had a little tent and chair at the top of the hill where he cut hair.

"I remember watching him a few times, looking here, looking there. He always acted like he wasn't doing anything, but you could tell that he was up to something," Simpson says. "You could see him walk over here, over there, like he was stepping off distances.

"I thought about him, what he was doing, and remember telling one of the newcomers in the unit that there was a good chance we're gonna get hit some day."

Roger Coffey was a medic with Headquarters Battery, but he had been assigned to Charlie Battery for so long, he felt like he was part of the original unit. That night, he was in his bunker, not too far from the maintenance area, which he shared with two cooks, Stanley Stone, who was on guard duty, and another medic, new in the unit, whose name no one remembers. This wasn't too smart. If the bunker was destroyed, both medics could be lost.

He heard the first explosion that night, jumped off his bunk, shouted "Incoming!" and felt his hand start to burn—a piece of shrapnel came through an opening and caught a finger.

"I grabbed my .45 and got on the ground in the entrance. The others were taking up positions at the other openings, and I could see people running around outside," he says.

Stanley Stone's guard bunker had a foot of water in it from the rainstorm they had earlier that evening. The bunker was small, dug mostly in the ground, with about three feet above ground. There was a small entrance in the rear, facing toward the battery and the guns. There was about four feet of ground outside the front of the bunker, then a hill going down.

Fred Osborne, who was on guard with Stanley Stone that night, was close by in the maintenance area. He didn't want to spend the night in a foot of water. Around one-thirty A.M., Stone heard a sucking sound, like when you step in mud, then pull your foot out. Very slowly, he inched his way to the small entrance at the back of the bunker, went out, and started to crawl slowly, quietly onto the roof. Then a North Vietnamese tossed a satchel charge that peeled the roof back like a tin can. Stone sailed up into the night, conscious, saw the mess hall on fire, other explosions and fires, came down, landed on his feet, just missing some stakes that were in the ground, and began to run toward the maintenance bunker, but he couldn't get there. "Someone threw a satchel charge at me from about ten feet away, then another. Soon there were explosions all around me. I just couldn't move. I was being hit with rocks and dirt, I couldn't go right or left, I couldn't turn around," he remembers.

"Then it let up for a few seconds, and I tried to get in the bunker for Gun 4. But three times I got close to the door, and each time I got blown back," he adds.

Then he decided to head for the bunker where he slept, which was about fifty feet away.

Roger Coffey was still on the ground in the doorway when a satchel charge sailed over his body and landed close by. But it didn't explode. Instead, there was some smoke and a terrible odor, and someone shouted, "Gas!" Coffey grabbed it and tossed it back outside, then got back in the doorway on the ground.

"I was looking out the door when I saw Gun 3 take a direct hit and explode. The back door blew off, and someone came running out totally on fire, then fell to the ground and didn't move," he says. "At that point, I didn't know if there were others in the gun or not."

Then another satchel charge was tossed over him, landed on the floor, and exploded. "One of the cooks got hit, the other medic got hit in the head, and I had my leg cut up with shrapnel and my hair was burned off," he says.

"The place was a shambles inside. I got back to the door, looked outside, and saw this gook up on the highest point on the hill, maybe one hundred fifty yards away, firing RPGs," Coffey recalls.

"Gun 3 was totally engulfed in flames now, and I figured the rest of the crew was still inside."

Stanley Stone, although knocked to the ground twice by the concussions from two satchel charges, got to his bunker and made it inside, but he might have been better off outside. No sooner had he gotten inside than an RPG tore through a wall, hit the top of a twelve-by-twelve-inch corner post, and exploded. Tiny bits of shrapnel peppered his head and back. The concussion lifted him off the ground and slammed him to the earth, facedown. He looked toward the wall where his guitar had been hanging, and all he could see was two strings. He got up, grabbed a rifle and a dozen or so clips, and took up a position at one of the doorways. A few minutes later, he saw a shape doubled over at the waist, heading straight for the door. He picked up an M-79 grenade launcher, pointed it at the shape, and started to squeeze the trigger ever so gently. A satchel charge went off close to the running shape and lit the area just long enough for Stone to see Fred Osborne making his way toward him, obviously in great pain.

"The adrenaline was so high, I just reached out and picked him up with one hand and got him inside and placed him against a wall," Stone says. Just about that time, an RPG penetrated the front wall, didn't explode, and went out the back wall, missing his head by no more than several inches.

"Later, I asked Fred if he remembered the rocket that whizzed by his face, and he said he never saw it," Stanley Stone recalls.

They placed Osborne on the floor, and Coffey gave him a shot of morphine, did what he could for his stomach wound, then went back to the front entrance.

"Oh, my God, they got Skippy's gun! They got Skippy's gun!" Coffey shouted.

"All I could think of was that they killed my brother," Stanley remembers.

"Stanley, they're runnin' out the back of the gun!" Coffey then shouted.

"Can you see my brother?"

"I can't say yes, I can't say no. I just see some guys runnin' out the back!" Coffey remained at one entrance, Stanley Stone at the other, trying to keep the shapes that were running by from getting close enough to toss in satchel charges. About a half hour later, when the gunfire and explosions had quieted somewhat, Skippy Stone, Stanley's brother, came in and told Coffey to get his medical bag. "We gotta get to the FDC, 'cause that's where they're takin' all the wounded." That's when the brothers, Skippy and Stanley Stone, knew the other was safe.

When Coffey got inside the Fire Direction Center, it was a

mess—mass confusion. It was full of wounded. Coffey saw Buck Harned, went over to him, and said, "Gosh darn, Buck, what the hell happened?"

"You wouldn't believe what ran over me," Harned answered.

"He always had a sense of humor, even then," Coffey remembers. Coffey wrapped Harned's wounds, gave him a shot of morphine, then moved on to other wounded. Bit Blanford was there. "I patched his leg, it was pretty bad, and gave him morphine."

Coffey next spotted Dan Doyle on the ground, bent over him to bandage his wounds, and asked, "Darn, what happened to you?"

"Am I alive? Am I alive?" Doyle asked.

"You're alive," Coffey reassured him.

Bad as his wounds were, Doyle was able to use the radio to contact Phu Bai, then give it to Coffey.

"I didn't follow procedure," Coffey remembers, "because I forgot what procedure was at that time. So I just said, 'This is the pill on the hill, this is the pill on the hill. We've got mass casualties and dead, and we need the pill out here.'" In other words, send a doctor and all the help you can.

"We need a lot of supplies," Coffey added.

"Be there in the morning."

"We need the pill, bad," Coffey stressed.

The helicopters were overhead in no time, but they wouldn't land because there was still a lot of gunfire on the hill.

"It looked like they were havin' a parade up there," Coffey remembers. Then Coffey heard over the radio: "We're coming down. Have the wounded on litters, and let's get 'em out of there."

Stanley Stone was still in the bunker when he heard the roar of Puff the Magic Dragon, the old C-47, then saw the stream of what looked like hot coals coming down on top of the North Vietnamese.

"I put my rifle down, lit a cigarette, and knew it was all over now," he says.

"Then I went out, took a look around the hill, saw the flag still flyin' full of holes, and thought what the guy who wrote that song must have felt," Stanley Stone remembers.

The crew of Gun 2 had just finished their missions for the

night and were taking a break outside the gun. They'd been firing "firecracker" rounds—projectiles with eighty small balls inside filled with tiny needles. If the round was set to explode above ground, the balls would hit the ground, bounce up, and explode, sending swarms of deadly needles in all directions.

Around one-thirty, Donnie Allender heard the explosion that blew up the mess hall. Then another explosion in the maintenance area. Both were at the top of the hill, the high end of the saddle. Then he heard someone running down from the hill, shouting, "Gooks in the mess hall!" The crew on duty jumped back in the gun and buttoned up the hatch, but the batteries in the gun that raise the tube were dead. So they had to hand-crank it up, then down, which took more time. When the tube was up, it was a perfect target for the RPGs. "The only thing that saved us is that the gun was in a horseshoe with dirt piled up around it and a two-and-a-half-ton truck right in front of it," Allender says. "When they tried to hit us from the front, they'd hit the truck, or the RPG would go over us.

"So the only chance they had to hit us was when the tube was up," he continues. It took three or four seconds to raise the tube using the batteries, between ten and fifteen seconds by hand. The crew stayed in their gun, firing every round they had, then all their illumination. Four of the six guns were either destroyed or put out of action.

In the first few minutes of the attack, the gun lost contact with the FDC. Then the crew began taking in stragglers from other guns that were burning. At first light, those who were not wounded took up guard positions around the perimeter in case the North Vietnamese returned, which many of the men thought they would do. Then Allender took a quick look at part of the hill.

"The wire bunker was completely destroyed," Allender says. "I think what really got it was when the North Vietnamese would shoot at our tube when it was up, miss, and hit right about where the wire bunker was. The wire bunker took a lot of RPG hits that were meant for us," he explains.

"The hill that morning was a mess, and the people were in shock," he adds.

A BAD HILL

It was close to first light when Don Parrish saw a shape that he recognized standing in the doorway. "It was still pitch-black, but I could see, with the help of a little light from the explosions, that Jim Moore was standing in the front opening," Parrish remembers, "and I knew he was in pain."

"Jim, are you okay?"

"Donald, I'm hurt. I'm burned up!" said Moore, whose gun was one of the first destroyed.

"At this point, I don't think Jim realized how badly he was burned," Tom Raisor says of his closest friend, who died a few days later on a hospital ship.

About this time, the North Vietnamese began to withdraw. They used flares of different colors to indicate to the assault force what they were supposed to do. "We think the guy with the flares used the wrong color," Parrish says. "A prisoner we captured later said that the flare used meant to withdraw. Instead, what they wanted to do was bring in fresh troops."

Puff the Magic Dragon had been overhead for thirty minutes, blasting anything that moved along the perimeter, anything that went into the jungle, anything that came out of the jungle. Puff carried an incredible amount of firepower. Four Gatling guns, each with several barrels, spewed out a stream of withering fire toward the enemy. Every fifth or sixth round was a tracer.

"It was a solid stream of red comin' down," Joe Keeling remembers. "It looked like [if] you'd take a bucket of red hot coals and pour 'em out continuously." Soon the sky overhead was full of Cobra gunships firing at the North Vietnamese as they fled into the jungle. Then a steady stream of evacuation helicopters began to descend, to take away the dead and wounded.

"Jim Moore gave up his seat on a helicopter for someone he felt was worse off," Lieutenant Lee remembers. "It amazed me. I couldn't believe what I was seeing."

Jerry Janes left aboard the last MedEvac helicopter just before first light that took the wounded to the hospital at Phu Bai.

"I gotta have your rifle," the gunner on the helicopter said to Janes.

"You don't get my rifle," Janes told him.

"I want your rifle," the gunner said, a little louder and a bit firmer than before.

Janes took the rifle off his shoulder, pointed it toward the ground, and said: "You don't get my rifle. Period. There's no more talk. You don't take my rifle!"

"I thought I was comin' back to Tomahawk, and at that point in time, I wasn't turnin' loose of that rifle," he explains.

When the helicopter touched down, Janes got off, with his rifle, and ran into a medic whose job it was to help walking wounded.

"I must have looked a sight. I didn't realize I had blood all over my back, my clothes were burned up. I looked a lot worse than I felt," Janes remembers.

The medic took one look at him and said, "You're going back to the world. But first, I gotta have your rifle."

"You don't get my rifle!"

Janes reached the hospital, all brick with concrete floors, and saw two men just outside wearing the hospital garb of orderlies.

"Hey, man, you're going' home. This trip will get you home," one of them said.

"I thought I'd be in there two or three days, get fixed up, and go back to the hill," Janes says. "So I got inside the hospital, and everyone was more interested in getting my rifle than fixin' me up.

"Then a WAC nurse got me. She hit me with a big needle back here and dropped me," Janes says. "I remember going' down, hitting' the floor, and grabbin' for my rifle that I'd dropped."

When he awakened, a doctor was working on his back, picking out bits of metal, trying to make certain that the burns did not become infected. Then the WAC nurse came in.

"How's your hip?"

"Sore. The way you hit me with that needle."

They laughed about it, then she told him he was going home as soon as they finished working on him.

"I saw Jim Moore while I was there," Janes recalls. "I asked the nurse about Jim, and she just shook her head. Rich Daley was there. Bill Kinder was there. Dan Doyle was there. So was Wayne Collins. Kinder and Daley died a few days later.

"I walked around the hospital, just started talkin' to people, so I knew who was dead, who was hurt bad." That Friday afternoon, he wrote his girlfriend, Joy Brooks, and gave her all the information he had about the men from Bardstown.

Janes was there for a few days, then was flown to a hospital in Japan, a burn center, because he had developed an infection, stayed there two weeks, and returned to Bardstown on July 4, 1969.

David Unseld heard about the attack on Tomahawk almost immediately. He and a few friends from the other two batteries in the Second Battalion who had also been transferred out borrowed a truck and drove down to Tomahawk the next day, but didn't see anyone they knew. "They didn't want anyone on the hill asking questions. It was pretty touchy, it was kinda like the hill was under quarantine," he remembers.

In October, Unseld rejoined his friends from Charlie Battery at Phu Bai, and they flew home together, shouting, and hollering. "We were about a half hour out of Louisville when the captain came on the intercom and said, 'We're over St. Louis, and we're expecting a little turbulence. . . .' Suddenly, the plane dropped, I don't know how far, but to me it seemed like a hundred feet," Unseld says.

"In one second, you could hear a pin drop," he recalls.

When Teddy Marshall heard about the attack on Tomahawk, he got a three-day pass, hitched a ride on a cargo plane, and landed at Phu Bai. But the flight was not without incident.

"There were about twenty of us on that plane, on what ordinarily would be a routine flight, but all of a sudden, I heard a very loud pop, and the radio operator jumps up, throws off his helmet, and runs to the rear of the plane, where there are seven parachutes," Marshall remembers. "I watch him put [one] on, then watch him start to work on the rear cargo door. You know, I thought he was gonna bail out. Now I'm thinkin', there's twenty of us, and I can see six parachutes, and I'm wonderin' how we're gonna work this out." The radio operator didn't bail out, though. He just went back there to crank tight the rear cargo door that had popped loose.

"It wasn't funny then, but I laugh about it today," he adds.

Marshall spent several hours with Charlie Battery, or what was left of it, then flew back to Chu Lai, and came home in October on the same plane with David Unseld, the flight that hit the air pocket and suddenly dropped. "That wasn't any fun either," he remembers.

"Death and destruction were everywhere that morning," Parrish says of the day of the attack. "It was a terrible sight. Enemy bodies were everywhere. I counted twenty-eight close by, and there were signs that the enemy had dragged many of their dead and wounded away.

"We checked our men to see who was still breathing, who had got hit, who had died. Five were killed from my area. I knew them well. Several were seriously wounded. Many had lesser wounds. Fires were still burning.

"I knew as soon as I went out that some of my friends had been killed. Already, rumors were flying. 'So and so had died.' 'So did . . .' 'What did you hear?' 'Is it true?' Then it began to sink in just how lucky we had been to survive," Parrish says.

"Then it all came back to us—what a terrible place to be. It couldn't be defended. All the bad things we had heard about—it caught up with us that night. They all came true," Parrish relates.

"It was just a bad hill," he adds. "We left it a short time later, and not long after that, it was abandoned forever."

"I thought we were going to be massacred that night," Jodie Haydon remembers.

"A few weeks earlier, an army chaplain reminded us of what had happened on Hamburger Hill—total annihilation—and told us to keep our guard up and never let that happen to us," Hayden says.

"Compounding the problem for us was absolutely no visibility. You couldn't see anything, absolutely nothing, on which to make a decision to do something," he explains. "I'm surprised there were not more dead on that hill, and I'm surprised that we did not have more night skirmishes."

In the morning, at first light, he helped carry wounded up to a knoll and then put them on helicopters. Then he slept for an hour. When he got his first clear look at the hill, the first thing he saw was the flag flying on top of the exec post.

"Whenever I hear the national anthem played or sung, I always see that flag," he remarks.

Of the war itself, he says, "The North Vietnamese had more will to win than we did."

Tom McClure got to the hill around eight-thirty A.M., and Parrish and McClure walked around the perimeter, surveyed the entire area, saw where the North Vietnamese had cut the wire in three locations.

"What the hell has happened here?" McClure wondered. "I can't believe this."

"I looked for guys I came over with. It was terribly depressing," he says. "I was thinking of the good times we had had. Why the hell did it have to happen. I was angry. After a few minutes, I tried to think why."

"My God, how did you survive?" McClure asked Parrish.

"I didn't know for sure myself, or how anyone survived that night, for that matter," Parrish says. McClure was amazed at the amount of damage.

"Who's been killed?" he asked Parrish.

"Four that I know of," Parrish replied. "I sent their names, ranks, and serial numbers over the radio at seven-thirty."

"There was no mistake. I knew them all. Yet when the information got back to Bardstown, two of them were listed as missing," he explains. "In fact, even myself and Jodie Haydon were reported as missing in action."

McClure and Parrish talked about the survivors, families, friends back home. "Jodie and I were worried about the effect this would have on everyone back home, because we knew what the news would say—Fire Base Tomahawk had been overrun, and several National Guardsmen had been killed and many others wounded," Parrish says.

"We rationalized that they'd just have to get by on rumors for a couple of days until we could write home and they could get solid information," Haydon adds.

In some instances, the military would inform a family that a son had been reported missing in action when it was known for certain that he had been killed. Then, a few days later, they would inform the family that their son had been killed in action. Regardless of the reason—accidental or intentional—this just added confusion to an already chaotic situation and further upset the people of Bardstown.

"The 101st was fighting right alongside us, and they suffered higher casualties than we did," Parrish says. "They had the key guard post on the western edge of the perimeter facing up a mountain, and four of the six men in that bunker were killed." The under-strength airborne platoon high on top of the other end of the saddle was eliminated as a fighting force, with most of the men dead or wounded.

"The enemy wanted our guns," Parrish says, "and they were gonna get them at any price. At the same time, they were also doing a lot of damage to the battery. They wanted to destroy the morale of the men, too. That was almost as important as getting the guns."

Later that morning, the battalion scrounged up three guns for the battery, taking them from the other firing batteries in the battalion. They also sent the men to fire them because Charlie Battery had lost a lot of men.

"It was very scary the night of June twentieth," Parrish remembers. "No one really slept, try as we might. All the guard posts were awake. They fired at a lot of shapes. They even got a few of the enemy."

Parrish was on the hill for two more days, then went to Tokyo on rest and recuperation leave, and it was most welcome, if for no other reason than he could call home and get the rumors straightened out. He went to Yokohama, saw some of the men from the hill who were in the military hospital there, then called home. Parrish's family had been on the way to church when they heard that Fire Base Tomahawk had been overrun, and that there were many casualties, but they didn't know any details—who had died, who was wounded, how seriously. Parrish now straightened that out, giving his parents the names of the dead and wounded.

"I sent my first letter home just before leaving on R and R. In it, I gave a blow-by-blow description of what happened, just to set the record straight," Parrish says.

"Mom told me on the phone that the town was very upset, that the people were very much disturbed. Others in town had heard from various sources that I was missing," he adds. "Fortunately, my mom hadn't heard this one, so she was greatly relieved when I called her."

When Parrish returned to Charlie Battery, it was just leaving the hill en route to Phu Bai, where it remained until October, when the unit returned to Bardstown. Parrish came home in early October with the advance party. It didn't take long for him to see that the mood of the town had changed so far as the war was concerned.

"Most of the people in town had had a basic support for the war. Some felt stronger about it than others, but just about everyone was in favor of what we were doing over there. It was later on that a lot of things came out and changed their minds," he says.

"I, at the time, felt it was the proper thing to do—that we were doing the right thing by being in Vietnam. But later, as I learned more, I wasn't so sure," he adds. "Now the town is questioning it a great deal, wondering why we were over there in the first place."

"It was one of the hardest jobs I ever had to do," Tom McClure remembers. "How do you tell a wife about her husband, a mother about her son? The men had been writing home pretty regular, so everyone back in Bardstown had a pretty good idea of what was going on over there. But at this point, we asked them not to write home until we had firsthand information as to just what had happened, who had been killed, wounded.

"We didn't want the people back home to get more excited than necessary," he adds. "Military policy is that first you tell next of kin that loved ones are missing in action. Then, formal notices came from Fort Knox, and a chaplain spoke with the next of kin. But many of them already knew because of the letters that the guys had written home.

"There was reason to believe that the enemy had eaten in the mess hall, that food had been carried from that mess hall," McClure says. "When we walked down the perimeter that following morning, we ventured out several hundred meters away from the fire base, and there were milk cartons that obviously were ours. In other words, some of them hadn't been there just that night, some of them had been there for a week or so."

Larry Johnson was in the hospital at Phu Bai for about ten days, then was sent to a much bigger hospital in Japan because his ankle wound had become infected. He never saw Tomahawk again.

"Well, I guess you're glad you're going home?" a medic remarked.

"I am?"

"Yep!"

Johnson was back in Louisville August 14, spent a few days at Fort Knox, then returned to Bardstown.

"Disbelief. Shock. Numbness. That was my personal feeling after seeing the hill at first light," Tom Raisor remembers. "I took one look and thought that we had probably lost half our men. That's how bad the damage was.

"Everybody was sort of stunned, people were running around trying to identify bodies, who was wounded, where had they been taken," he says. "There was total numbness on the hill that morning.

"You were just thankful that you were alive," Raisor recalls.

Raisor went to the hospital that morning to see what was causing that ringing in his head—it was a concussion, but not serious—and he returned to the hill in a few hours.

"Two days later, I wrote Mom and Dad. I could imagine what was being said. So I wrote back and told them that I was okay, that we had a little bit of a problem, but that we'd be okay, and not to worry.

"My dad was at the police station talking to some friends about something when it came over the wire that I had been injured, so someone there walked over to Dad and said, 'I don't know how to tell you this, but your son has been injured in Vietnam.'

"When my mom found out, I think she was almost in hysterics.

"We think that David Collins surprised the North Vietnamese, forcing them to prematurely begin their attack, before they could all get in position around the bunkers and guns," Raisor explains.

"I think that there were supposed to be several of the enemy around each bunker and each gun, and on a given signal, hurl satchel charges inside. But because they were surprised in the mess hall, they had to begin their attack before everyone was in position," Raisor adds.

"David Collins probably saved a bunch of our lives," he says.

The men on Fire Base Tomahawk withstood around 150 RPGs and satchel charges and heavy fire from AK-47s. The North Vietnamese destroyed three howitzers (a fourth could not be fired), an ammunition storage area, nine bunkers, the mess hall, the dining tent, the maintenance area, four ammunition carriers, three two-and-a-half-ton trucks, two three-quarter-ton trucks, and three jeeps. Ten men in Battery C were killed that night. The five Guardsmen were Luther Chappel, David Collins, Ronnie McIlvoy, Jim Moore, and Ronnie Simpson. The five regular army men who had infused into the battery and were killed that night were Troy Bethea, Washington; Harold R. Christensen, California; Gerald C. Daley, New Jersey; Larry W. Kinder, Virginia; and William J. Kuhns, Missouri. About forty-five were wounded. Between twenty-five and thirty North Vietnamese were killed, probably many more, because numerous trails of blood led into the jungle, and there were many markings on the ground to indicate that bodies had been dragged away. About thirty-six hours later, a wounded North Vietnamese was found below the hill. He told his captors that two days earlier, the Vietnamese force had practiced its attack on Tomahawk on a hill close by. He said also that a full battalion had originally been scheduled to carry out the assault, but at the last minute, the number of men in the attacking force had been reduced.

"Most of the people killed that night were either outside their bunkers or inside their guns," Raisor says.

"There was probably some complacency with us all in the fact that we didn't keep our small arms with us at all times, particularly at night, because that's when we were the most vulnerable," he adds. "I always had my rifle in the bunker where I slept, or in the FDC, where I worked, but when I went to the mess hall, or anyplace else on the hill, I never did take it with me.

"After the attack, you couldn't have pried those rifles out of their hands. They all had their flak jackets on, steel helmets, too, and everyone carried a bandolier of clips for the M-16," he continues.

"But that was like shutting the door after the cat was out," Raisor adds.

"It was just a bad hill to defend," Ronnie Hibbs says. "For one, the guard bunkers were too far apart. On a rainy night, you could drive a car between them with the lights on, and we'd probably never know it."

Vigilance in the guard bunkers seemed to be a problem. Even the night after the attack, Charles Stone and his brother, Stanley, checked a perimeter bunker and found the men, both newcomers, asleep.

Over the months, the gun crews had developed a few habits that were questionable. They would hand-ram the projectiles into the tube rather than use the hydraulic-power rammer, which took a second longer. But with practice, you could make that second up.

Some of the crews were not swabbing the tube after every firing, as they were supposed to do. After a projectile is fired, a residue of powder remains in the tube, smoldering. When you put in another projectile, then the powder, there is a chance the powder will explode.

Tom Eatmon, who had gone on leave, was in Hawaii with his wife when he ran into an officer from another battery in the battalion.

"Did you hear about Charlie Battery?" he asked Eatmon.

"No!"

"They got overrun."

"My heart liked to jump out of my throat. I couldn't get back there fast enough," Eatmon says. He got back two days later, arriving on top of Tomahawk after dark, around nine-thirty P.M. Around one A.M., a trip flare went off. "You never heard so much shooting. Everyone opened up in that direction," he recalls. He was elated.

"They finally got it," he remembers thinking. "That's what Danny and I had been tryin' to drill into them."

"The thing that saved Charlie Battery was their training, and the things they did on their own," Eatmon adds.

Tom Raisor knew that Jim Moore had died aboard a hospital ship. He didn't know that he would be taking his body back to Bardstown. He found that out when the company commander told him, "You've been selected as body escort for Jim Moore. Don't worry about anything. Just get your gear together and be back here in a few minutes, and I'll have someone take you to Phu Bai." This was five days after the attack, and he was back at work in the Fire Direction Center after spending four hours in the hospital at Phu Bai.

"I was told to tell the dispatcher at the airport there that I'm a body escort and that I need to get to Oakland, California," Raisor says.

"Well, if you'll just have a seat over there," the dispatcher told him, pointing to several benches. It was already dark, Raisor really hadn't had any sleep since the attack on the hill, so he stretched out on the bench and tried to get a little rest. His eyes hadn't been closed for more than a few minutes when the dispatcher came over, shook him awake, and said, "There's a plane out there, just go out and get on it."

"It was a cargo plane, there were no seats in it, so I just sat in the cargo bay," Raisor says. "Then the pilot and copilot got aboard, saw me back there, and motioned me forward."

"Come on up here with us," the pilot said.

Raisor told them that he was a body escort, and they told him what to do as soon as they touched down at Cam Ranh Bay.

"Get your money changed to American currency, tell 'em you're a body escort and that you need to get to Oakland, California. That's all you need to remember," they told Raisor.

"When I got there, the first thing I did was tell someone at the ticket window that I was a body escort and I need to get to Oakland, California," he relates.

"Go over and get your money changed, and I'll take care of the rest," a woman at the ticket counter told him.

"I was getting my money changed when they paged me, so I ran back to the ticket window, and the woman pointed to a little door, and said, 'There'll be a jeep outside the door, and you just get in it.'

"So I ran out the door, jumped in the jeep, and they're driving me down the runway like all get-out," he says. "Then I see this big Braniff jetliner parked at the end of the runway. They'd stopped the plane so I could get aboard. I stood on the top of the windshield and was pulled into the airliner, and we then took off.

"It was loaded when I got aboard, and they were all cheering and yelling because they were going home for good," Raisor remembers.

He went from Cam Ranh Bay to Guam, then to Fort Lewis, Washington, where the flight ended.

At each stop, he simply told someone in charge that he was a body escort, and things always seemed to work out. All he had with him were the clothes he wore—his jungle fatigues. "At Fort Lewis, I got dress greens, so I could get something to eat in the commissary, then I got a flight to San Francisco. I just kept telling everyone who asked a question, 'I'm a body escort, and I need to get to Oakland, California,' " he says.

As soon as he landed at San Francisco, he went to the military detachment there and was given a shuttle vehicle and a driver who drove him to the army base at Oakland.

It was late at night when Raisor arrived. He didn't know where he was supposed to go, so they drove around and around until he saw a light on, a door open, and spotted an officer—a captain.

He said those magic words, and the captain said, "Well, we have a holding area to keep all the body escorts in one place, so I'll take you there."

He showed Raisor where to sleep, where the mess hall was.

"I went to school for two days on how to be a body escort," Raisor says.

"Basically, you were taught how to conduct yourself in a manner that wouldn't be disgraceful to the family and the military," he explains. "They gave you a flag, taught you how to fold it, how to put it on the coffin, how to keep it on the coffin so that it wouldn't fall off, and [gave you] a black armband to wear when you were in the presence of the coffin. And [you did] a lot of paperwork."

When he was through with school, he was told to go back to his barracks and, except for eating, to stay there because they didn't know when he would be needed.

"Well, about two o'clock in the morning, a major and a colonel came and woke me up," Raisor recalls.

"It's time to go," one of them said.

"It was almost like you see in the movies with secret agents doing all these strange things, always talking low, hushed tones," he remarks. "I guess it was just being respectful, but it was kind of scary."

The two officers drove Raisor back to San Francisco in a big, black limousine. When they got to the airport, the one not driving said, "When we get to the area where the coffins are assembled, you will have to identify the body that you are to escort. Once you've identified it, you put your flag on it, and stay with it until it has been loaded on the plane."

The body had to be loaded feet first. Any time it was moved, it had to be moved feet first. "If they moved it head first, I was supposed to make a report and call a certain number and report that they hadn't handled the body properly," Raisor says. "Any time the plane stopped, even if passengers got on or off, the body had to be taken off, then put back on, even if it was the same plane."

The American Airlines jet was full. Raisor was the only body escort; there was only one coffin aboard.

"When we landed at Dallas, I went up to the stewardess and told her, 'I'm a body escort and . . .' and she knew what to do." Raisor got off and was led to the area of the plane where the coffin was. "They were waiting until I got there, then they took it off, and I placed the flag on top. When it was time to go, they put the coffin on the plane, I folded up my flag, and then I went back to my seat." The plane landed again at Nashville, and they went through the same routine again.

"I guess they took such great care with the body because if something happened to the plane on the ground, they didn't want anything to happen to the body," Raisor says.

"When we got to Louisville, a funeral parlor from Bardstown had a hearse waiting, so we placed the coffin in it, and I rode with the coffin back to Bardstown," Raisor adds. Jim Moore was finally going home.

FOUR

A Town in Agony

I t was easy to overlook. In fact, most residents of Bardstown did just that. It was little more than an inch in length and appeared near the end of a detailed news story in the *Louisville Times* the evening of June 19, 1969, describing what had occurred that day in the war in Vietnam:

". . . elite North Vietnamese commandos trained in demolition penetrated an artillery base 30 miles northwest of South Vietnam's second largest city and hurled satchel charges. The commandos moved in behind a barrage of 150 mortar shells that pinned down American paratroopers of the 101st Airborne Division defending Fire Base Tomahawk. Two paratroopers were killed and 24 wounded."

Deanna Simpson, Mary Collins, Betty Stone, and Joy Brooks, now Mrs. Jerry Janes, were among the very few who did not overlook that buried paragraph.

"I read the paper that day, and there was just a paragraph or two that said that Fire Base Tomahawk had been attacked and that they took heavy casualties," Joy Janes says. "For some reason, I mistook what it really said, and I thought that the casualties were the men in the 101st. Normally, I would have been petrified, but for some unknown reason, my mind just blocked out what the story said; it just didn't sink in.

"Beverly Cecil, a good friend, and I discussed that newspaper story in class that night and further convinced ourselves that the casualties were in the 101st Airborne," she says. "We convinced ourselves that none of our men were hurt. I realize now how stupid that was, but we were only protecting ourselves."

By nightfall, though, the telephones were beginning to ring all over town.

"Did you read that story in the newspaper?"

"Have you heard anything about our men being attacked?"

Late that night, many of the people in town were aware of the story in the *Times,* but few knew much else. The attack was mentioned briefly on the late night news, but what was said was coming from the story in the newspaper.

"That newspaper story was the first inkling I had that anything had happened over there," Mary Collins remembers, and she discussed it with a few friends.

"We knew at that time they were splitting up the unit, moving some of our guys out, moving new men in, so we thought maybe our guys weren't on the hill at that time, or maybe it was the wrong hill," she says. "Maybe they weren't affected, because we hadn't received any information of any kind, and since we hadn't heard anything, well, we figured that no news is good news.

"And then we heard about Jim Moore," Mary continues.

Word reached Bardstown the next day, Friday, that Moore had been badly injured and that he had been transferred to a hospital ship where communications were much better than at the army hospital at Phu Bai, where most of the wounded from Fire Base Tomahawk had been taken. The improved communications network aboard ship probably explains how Mrs. Moore learned that her husband had been injured about two days before the identities of the other casualties became known.

As soon as word spread that Moore had been injured, Mary Collins and Betty Stone went to see his wife, who had two young children at home. "She really didn't know a whole lot," Mary remembers, "but she was very upset.

"At that time, we did not know if any others had been killed or wounded, but nevertheless, I was a nervous wreck, I was so worried and concerned, because now we knew our boys were involved," Mary says.

"A friend called Friday and told me that the unit had been overrun, but that's all anyone knew for some time," Lorraine Stumph remembers. "After that call, it was just waiting for any details, to see who had been hurt, because we had heard later on the news that there had been casualties.

"Friday afternoon, I found out that Jim Moore had been hit, then all the women began calling each other, trying to put this thing together," Lorraine says.

"The telephone was pretty hot back then," she adds.

"I was very sad, very concerned, and that seemed to be the mood of the town," says Lorraine, whose husband, Bobby, was caught in the attack.

Betty Stone, who also read the news story, and whose husband, Charles, was in one of the gun crews on Tomahawk that was hit hard, remembers the telephone call Thursday night, June 19, from Kenny Ice, who had returned to Bardstown because his duty time in Charlie Battery was up.

"He asked if I had heard anything, or knew anything about the men in the unit," Betty recalls. "I told him I hadn't received any word from my husband, or anyone else."

Then she asked him: "Kenny, were they in a bad position?"

"Well, yes," he said, then explained that the gun battery was situated on a very low hill, with much higher hills around it.

"I guess I'm lucky," said Ice, who completed his six-year enlistment and came home May 9.

"When I left there, only twenty percent of the Bardstown unit was to be left together at the last of June," he adds.

"After that, I took my son, Chris, and went out to see Charlie's mom and dad, and told them about the situation. I told them that I thought it surely was our men who had been attacked," Betty says, "but we didn't hear anything else for a few days."

Then she went home and waited for the telephone to ring. Waited for word from anywhere, anyone, that would shed some light on the fate of the men on Fire Base Tomahawk. She didn't call any of the other wives that night and tell them what she had read.

Nelson County Deputy Sheriff Raffo Wimsett delivered a telegram from the secretary of the army to Patsy Moore at eleven P.M. Saturday, June 21, officially notifying her that her husband, Sgt. James Moore, had been badly burned.

The telegram read: "Your husband, wounded in action in Vietnam, June 19, while at artillery firing position when the area came under attack by hostile force, received second and third degree burns over 90 percent of his body. Placed on the very seriously ill list and in judgment of the attending physician, his condition is such that there is cause for concern."

"I think Patsy Moore was the first one to call me, probably Sunday morning. [She] told me that her husband, Jim, had been burned over ninety percent of his body," Betty Stone relates. "I think she said the sheriff had brought her a telegram early that morning." Betty then went out to visit Patsy and stayed there most of the morning. Then she stopped by Holly Bischoff's house. By Monday morning, word had spread all over Bardstown, throughout Nelson County, that Charlie Battery had been virtually destroyed as a fighting unit and that there was an untold number of dead and wounded.

"Anytime someone drove up the driveway, you thought they were coming to tell you someone had been killed, or wounded," Betty Stone says. "It was a very scary feeling.

"When I went to bed, I said a prayer that I wouldn't dream," she adds.

The war in Vietnam was now exacting a steady, deadly toll among young men in the Bardstown area. Raymond S. Ford, February 20, 1966; William Russell Taylor, August 28, 1966; William David Price, March 18, 1968; Albert William Hawkins, May 17, 1968; James Rafael Norris, November 3, 1968; and Harold M. Brown, who was killed by rocket fire while in a bunker at Chu Lai on June 11, 1969. He had been in the Guard for five years, in Vietnam for eight months, and only recently had transferred to a regular army unit.

Brown was the sixth young man from Bardstown, the surrounding area, or Charlie Battery to die so far in the Vietnam fighting.

By this time, many of the older people in town, mostly the parents of young people of draft age, were beginning to wonder what was going on over there. Why does the military continue to take our young people, then send them back to us in boxes? Why aren't we winning? If we aren't going to fight to win, let's get out of there.

"As time passed and the dead were coming home, the older people seemed to swing over to the position that the younger people had," remembers Mozena Cecil, now Mrs. Tom Raisor.

"I think when the war first started, it was something that was happening to everybody else, but not to you," she adds. "It was a war that you saw on television. Somebody else was over there doing the fighting, but then when people you know were over there doing the fighting, it hit home, it made a big difference in your thinking.

"Drugs in California are okay as long as the drugs stay there, but when it comes to Kentucky, to your town, then you are not too happy," she explains. "That's the way it was with the war."

For the people of Bardstown, for the women with loved ones in Charlie Battery, it was a terrifying period that would only get worse. Bad news travels fast in a small town, and in no time at all, everyone knew that Moore had been badly injured in Vietnam. Townspeople were beginning to feel that something terrible had happened to the men, but they didn't know just what.

"The first I heard about the fighting on the hill was maybe a day later, when Margaret Tobin called me," Mozena Raisor remembers. "She told me that her cousin, Jimmy Moore, had been wounded. My husband, Tom, and Jim had been close friends since childhood.

"I could tell that she was very upset over the phone when she called me that afternoon. Jimmy's mother, Margaret's aunt, had called and told her about his being wounded. I think she got it over the phone from the army," Mozena explains.

"Jimmy was married, so I immediately went over to see his wife, Patsy, who had two young children. At that time, they were living with Jim's parents," she adds.

"She was visibly upset. She was shaken, really shaken. As soon as I got out of the car, I could see that she was, more or less, in a state of shock," Mozena recalls. "We really didn't say much. I hugged her, and we went into the house. Jimmy's parents were there, and they were very upset, too. They knew only that he was wounded, nothing else.

"I stayed about an hour with Patsy. I really don't remember

anything else. I just hugged her. There were tears. Patsy was stunned, dazed, and I really didn't know what to do," she adds.

"Friday night, Holly Bischoff and I heard that Jim Moore had been burned," Joy Janes remembers, "but we couldn't make the connection between the attack and Jim Moore being burned. We thought that perhaps he had been in a truck accident. At this point, it was total confusion in Bardstown. Rumors abounded."

Patsy Collins remembers, "I was at David's mother and daddy's house when I first heard that the unit was attacked. It was a Sunday afternoon, and we heard a little bit about it on television, that something had happened over there.

"That's when the phone started ringing, different people calling everybody else to see if they knew any more," she says.

"It was one ring after another. I don't remember talking to anybody, but his brother's wife, Mary, came out, and she brought a little bit more information. But nobody seemed to know anything other than they had been hit," Patsy relates.

"But we kept thinking that none of them had been hit, that maybe they got their hills mixed up, that maybe it was another hill, so we all stayed there for a while, hoping we could find out more information," she adds. "Later, some of the wives got together, and we went from one house to another to see if there was any word about what happened, but there wasn't."

The people of Bardstown spent that weekend, June 21–22, seeking bits of information, trying to fit together pieces of what was rapidly becoming a deadly puzzle. Nervous, worried, very concerned would be the best way to describe the town at that time.

By late Sunday night, very little was known about Fire Base Tomahawk or the men of Charlie Battery, who were up there. No solid information was learned until first light, Monday, when two officers from nearby Fort Knox arrived in town bearing grim news.

It stormed all night. Many roads were flooded. Strong winds had toppled trees, and a number of roads were blocked. Patsy Collins and her son, Todd, who had been born April 13, were asleep in the upstairs bedroom of her parents' home. Rather than be home alone with an infant, she was staying with her family for a few months. It was around five-thirty A.M. and still raining, but the rain was beginning to taper off. Patsy's mother was up. So was her younger brother, Connie, who was getting ready to milk the cows. Her mother heard a car in the driveway.

Patsy was still asleep when her brother came up to awaken her.

"Put some clothes on and come downstairs, Patsy," her brother said.

"Why?"

"Mother said to put some clothes on," he explained.

"Why?"

"Mother wants you to put your clothes on and come down," her brother said again.

"I knew then that something was wrong," Patsy said.

"I put a housecoat on and started down. Just as soon as I rounded the curve in the middle of the stairs, I could see them standing there, and I knew that something bad had happened. How bad, I didn't know, but I knew that it was bad."

She gripped the railing a little tighter to steady herself, leaned against it for support, and came down slowly, knowing that when she reached the two men standing just inside the front door, she would find out just how bad it was.

The officers stood there, ramrod-straight, not a wrinkle in their uniforms.

"When I reached them, they identified themselves. One was a chaplain, and he told me," she says.

"Your husband, David, has been killed, and his brother Wayne has been wounded and is in critical condition. We don't have any other details," the chaplain said.

She remembers their asking her not to call David's parents until they could get out there and tell them. In a few minutes, they were gone.

"After that, everything was just a blur, and I was more or less in shock," she says. "I do remember my mother went into the kitchen to make breakfast because there's not a lot you can do in a situation like this; it's just something you have to face.

"My mother then took me out to see David's parents, and we were there for a little while, but exactly how long, I can't remember," she says. "I do remember they took it very, very hard.

"At that time, we thought that only David had been killed," Patsy continues. "We wanted to ask if others had died, but I don't think any of us asked.

"You know, when I was at David's parents' house the day before, his mother and I had convinced ourselves that it was another unit that had been attacked," she says.

"David always wrote back, saying, 'You know, there's no danger here, we're not in a danger zone, there's no fighting going on here.' I guess a lot of the wives were told that," Patsy remembers, "so it wasn't as if he was being shot at all the time.

"So I wasn't prepared for those two officers," she adds.

"My little world came to an end in just a few seconds that Monday morning," Patsy Collins remembers.

"There's a whole lot of what happened back then that I still don't remember. Parts of it will come back, like when I talk about it, but I just can't put it all together. It's almost like a loss of memory," she says. "But it's something you think about every day. I mean, there's not a day goes by that I don't think about it."

The armed forces, through numerous wars stretched over many years, have had plenty of opportunity, and time, to set up a system for notifying next of kin should someone die or even get wounded, while on duty.

Basically, there are two men on a notification team, usually an officer and an enlisted man, but not always. Quite often, one of them is a chaplain. Usually, they come from the closest military base. They make certain they are talking to the next of kin, be it a wife, mother, or father. They are instructed to ask the woman to first sit down, because she might faint. They prefer to do it out of the presence of children. Wives and mothers are expected to cry. If they do, the team calls a neighbor if the situation seems to be getting out of hand. The only thing they must say is, "The secretary of the army has asked me to inform you . . ." If the individual was in the navy or marine corps, condolences would be extended on behalf of the secretary of the navy, if in the air force, on behalf of the secretary of the air force. What the notification team member says next is up to that person, just as long as it expresses feeling, deep regret. Some are cold and professional. Others are warm and tender. And notification can be made only between the hours of six A.M. and ten P.M. Even so, there are still big cracks in the system.

Mary Collins heard a car pull into the driveway about six-thirty A.M. Monday. "I looked out and saw one man get out, and I knew that something had happened," she says. "My first thought was that Wayne had been killed, because I didn't think the army would send someone to tell me anything else." At that time, she and her newborn son were living with her parents. So her father went to the door and let the officer in.

"He told me that Wayne had been wounded," Mary remembers, "but I thought, 'Something's wrong here. Why would they come and tell me that?'"

"I knew that they didn't come and tell you that someone was wounded," she remembers thinking.

"How seriously?" she asked the officer.

"He has chest wounds."

"At that time, that's all they really knew," she says.

"But his brother David has been killed," the chaplain added.

Mary recalls that he said he'd just come from Patsy's house and told her, but that he hadn't been to talk to Wayne's parents, yet.

"I want to go with you when you tell his parents," Mary told him.

Mary got dressed and asked the officer if she could call other members of the family, but he said he would rather she didn't do that because they might get there before he could talk to the parents.

She got in the army sedan, and they drove to the Collins home on Plum Run Road. "The whole time I was going out there, I was praying that they would all be in the house, that they wouldn't see us coming, just driving up," Mary adds. About a mile from the Collins farm, the road was blocked by a large tree, so they had to walk the rest of the way.

"I went to the door, knocked, and we went in," Mary says.

"I don't even remember the officer's name, or even what he looked like . . . , but he then told them about their sons," she adds.

"Your son David has been killed, and your other son, Wayne, has been wounded," the officer said. He told the parents what little he knew about the death of David and the wounding of Wayne. He mentioned, also, that Ronnie Simpson was listed as missing in action. He remained there a short time, then left. There were other stops he had to make that terrible Monday.

"The only thing that I remember after that is that I got on the phone and began calling other members of the family," Mary says.

Patsy Collins and her mother arrived a short time later. Mary remained there the rest of the day. "We never were able to find out what Wayne's condition was the rest of that day, or get any details on when David's body would be coming home," Mary says.

Mary left briefly and told the grandparents what had happened to David and Wayne.

"Then I called work and told them that I wouldn't be there that day, and they said, 'Yes, we know, we've already heard.'

"By that time, the news had spread all over town," Mary says.

In minutes, telephones all over town were ringing, carrying the devastating news to wives, parents, girlfriends. David Collins was dead. Wayne Collins was seriously wounded. Jim Moore was badly burned. Luther Chappel, Charlie Battery's first sergeant, was dead. Ronnie McIlvoy and Ronnie Simpson were reported to be missing in action, although the men on Fire Base Tomahawk knew that both were dead.

Would there be more?

"I went to visit Holly Bischoff, then Mary Collins," Betty Stone says. "I went to see Deanna Simpson, but all I remember is that she was about to have her baby.

"We were all so afraid. It was just scary," Betty adds.

"There was a pounding at my door that woke me up," Holly Bischoff remembers. "I was afraid it was going to wake up my daughter, Shannon, too, so I went down and opened it. It was Vicky, Mary Collins's youngest sister, and she was crying."

"Holly, can I come in and stay with you?" she asked as she wiped away the tears.

"Vicky, my Lord, what's the matter?"

"Things at my house are horrible, everyone's crying, I can't stay there anymore," explained Vicky, who was seven at the time.

"What's the matter? What's happened?"

"David is dead, and Wayne is hurt bad," said Vicky.

"Vicky really didn't understand what was going on, so I kept her for a few hours, until someone came over and got her," Holly says.

"At that point, I began to realize for the first time that not everyone would be coming home," Holly remembers.

"I wanted to go over and talk to Mary, to be with her, but at the same time, I didn't want to intrude on a family that was grieving," she continues.

"I got on the phone and called Joy. I knew nobody would call her because she wasn't married," Holly remembers. "And I asked her to come stay with me because I was afraid."

Joy was home in bed when she first heard for certain that Charlie Battery had been overrun and that there were dead and wounded.

"My mother came in early Monday morning and said, 'Holly wants you on the phone,' so I knew that something was bad, or she wouldn't have called me that early," Joy remembers.

"Joy, can you come over and stay with me? I'm frightened. Two men from Fort Knox are in town telling who's been killed and wounded," said Holly, whose husband, Kent, was the supply sergeant with Charlie Battery. Normally, he was stationed back at Phu Bai, but there was the chance that he could have been on the hill the night of the attack.

"I'll be right there," Joy told Holly. But first, she called the post office and asked Neal Cornett if he would call her if he saw a letter from her boyfriend, Jerry Janes. Then she gave him the phone number at Holly's house. Once they were together, they began calling other women in town, trying to find out if they had heard anything, such as the names of others who may have been killed or wounded. Around two P.M., Joy got a call from Neal Cornett, who told her, "You've got a letter from Jerry."

"I'll be right down," she said. She picked up the letter and returned to be with Holly, and they shared its contents and talked for a while. Then Joy took it to Jerry's parents, then to the parents of Jodie Haydon, who was mentioned in it. Then she went to see a very close friend, Ann Ballard. After that, she went home and showed it to her parents.

Janes's letter, written the day after the attack from the military hospital at Phu Bai, said, in effect, "Well, I guess you've heard the news. I was injured and am in the hospital now." Then he listed the names of those from the Bardstown area who died, those who were injured. He also cleared up the question about one person who was listed as missing in action, Ronnie Simpson, whom Janes knew had been killed.

"It took an average of five days to get a letter from Jerry," Joy Janes remembers, "but when he was wounded, the letter got here in three days. It was as if God wanted it that way."

Later that afternoon, Patsy Moore went to see Holly Bischoff. "She told me that Jim had been burned and asked me what I thought," Holly recalls. "Well, we didn't know that burns could become worse as you went along, so I remember reassuring her that if he's lived this long, he's going to be all right." He died the next day.

That Monday night, Holly called Joy again and said, "I've got the best news I've had in a long time. They're sending Jerry home."

"I don't know how she found out," Joy says, "but I was elated. I guess her husband, Kent, called and told her."

Bardstown was in a terrible state of mind by this time. Everywhere you turned, you saw grief. Everyone seemed to be closely connected, in one way or another, to the men who had died on Fire Base Tomahawk, to those who had been wounded.

Then the official telegrams from the Department of the Army began to arrive, expressing regrets over the loss of a loved one. Then came the telegrams informing parents or wives that a son or husband had been wounded.

"People actually positioned themselves at the roads leading into Bardstown from Fort Knox, and if an army sedan with two officers in it showed up, they'd call ahead to alert the townspeople that more bad news was coming," Holly says. "Then someone would follow them to see where they stopped, and it wasn't but ten minutes later that the whole town knew about it."

Holly stayed home the rest of that day, afraid to leave, to be away from the telephone. She thirsted for news about the men in Charlie Battery. The other wives, the parents, remained at home that day, too, hoping for word of a loved one, yet afraid to answer the phone, or go to the front door, or even look out the front window if they heard a car in the driveway.

Ronnie McIlvoy's father, Joseph, was at work in the General Electric plant in Louisville when a friend came by and asked, "Joe, did you hear about the attack on the Guard unit?"

"I hadn't heard a word until then," he said, "and it was three or four more days until I heard any details."

Young McIlvoy's wife, Elaine, had just returned from summer school. She stopped at the mailbox, went around to the back of the house, and sat down in the kitchen to read a letter from her husband.

"He said he was safe, everything was fine, there was no fighting where he was, and that he was hoping his battalion would be pulled back and sent home early, because there were rumors this was happening to other units," the former Mrs. McIlvoy remembers.

Then she heard the knock on the back door.

"The army uniforms signaled that something was wrong," she says.

"Then the chaplain told me that my husband was reported missing in action, and they were gone," she recalls. They were on their way to talk to McIlvoy's parents.

"I called my sister, and she came over and took me out to see his parents," she continues. "I really didn't know what to think. I was afraid, very worried."

His father was at work. So was his mother. So the two officers went next door and told a neighbor that the McIlvoys' son was reported as missing in action in Vietnam. Then the neighbor contacted Dorothy McIlvoy, Ronnie's mother, at the sewing factory in Harrodsburg where she worked.

Four days later, the two officers returned and informed Elaine McIlvoy that her husband was no longer missing, that he had been killed in action. Then the army sent a telegram to his parents with the same information.

"It was devastating, simply devastating," Joseph McIlvoy remembers. "His mother and I think about it every day. It's never far away."

"We had two other children at that time, Nancy, twenty-one, and Tommy, eighteen, and they both took it very hard," Dorothy McIlvoy says.

"The whole town, the entire area, was very upset about what had happened to the boys over there, to our boys," Ronnie's father remembers, "and the telephones were very, very busy."

"This was a bad time for Bardstown. It was a bad time for anyone to wear a uniform here. It meant they were from Fort Knox and bringing bad news. If you heard a knock on your door, it meant someone was hurt or had been killed," Tom Raisor's wife, Mozena, says.

"It was a time when no one wanted to go to the door, or pick up the telephone. I guess a lot of us thought this would keep the bad news from us. It didn't.

"The mood in this town then was one of fear, worry, great concern, fear of what we would find out next. The entire town was very upset," she continues.

"Once we found out something for certain, then we would go to that person's house to see what they needed, to help where we could, to bring a shoulder to cry on, or just listen to them," Mozena adds.

"We were all just beginning to make a life for each other, raise families, to plan our futures, then this had to happen. All of a sudden, these people are gone out of our lives, some never to come back," she says. "It was a horrible time.

"People almost fainted at the sight of a uniform then," she recalls.

"I remember that when Tommy came home, he went to Bucky Ice's house to talk to his mom and dad about what happened on the hill," Mozena says. "He was in uniform when he knocked on the door, and Mrs. Ice almost fainted, until she realized who it was. She thought it was the army bringing her bad news."

Deanna Simpson also read that very brief account of the attack on Fire Base Tomahawk. But even before she read that news story, the night before the assault by North Vietnamese commandos, she had a strong feeling, a premonition, that her husband, Ronnie, was in trouble. Then, Friday morning, she heard a little more about the attack on the radio, but no names, no casualties were mentioned. Later that day, she received a letter from her husband in which he told her that he was fine, that he was in no danger. Like the rest of the wives, she heard nothing about the attack on Saturday or Sunday. Nevertheless, she had the feeling that something bad had taken place, that something was not right.

"I was laying down on the bed Monday morning, looking out the window," she remembers. "I had a clear view of the road leading up to the house. Then I saw the army car coming around the corner.

"I knew they were coming to see me," Deanna says. "Then two men got out, knocked, and came in and told me that Ronnie was missing in action.

"I couldn't figure out why they told me he was missing, because I knew he was dead, I could feel it," she remembers. "I just felt that he was dead. I knew it the night before I read about the attack in the paper.

"Sometimes I know that something has happened even before it happens," she explains. "It happened once, later, with my daughter. I knew of an incident even before she told me about it. It's happened a few other times, too.

"I found out Monday morning that David Collins had been killed even before they came to see me. Afterward, I found out about Jim Moore, that he had been burned," she continues. Later, she found out that Jim Moore had died.

"I was pregnant at the time, I was overdue, I was upset. So I didn't go anywhere, I couldn't go anywhere, I couldn't go see the other wives, but I did talk to Patsy Collins on the phone," Deanna Simpson explains.

At that time, she was living with relatives in Bardstown. Her family lived several miles from town, the road was hilly, there were many curves, so her husband felt that it would be best if she stayed in town until the baby was born.

It was, by far, the most traumatic period in her life, and her grief ran very deep. "My mother-in-law told me that my hurt in losing Ronnie was never as bad as hers, because he was her son," Deanna recalls. "Maybe she was right.

"I felt like they [the army] knew that he was dead," she says. "As far as my condition was concerned, being pregnant, what difference would it make if they told me then or waited one day, or two days? Did they think I would be stronger?

"On Wednesday, the two army men came back and told me

that Ronnie had been killed," she says. "I didn't say anything. I just listened.

"Later, this nice young soldier from Fort Knox came over to help me with paperwork, social security, GI insurance, Ronnie's personal belongings," she relates. "This went on for a few days, then one day he was killed in an automobile accident, so they had to send someone else over."

Pat Allender, who married her husband, Donnie, while Charlie Battery was in Texas, first heard about the attack on Monday, three days after it occurred. Pat, who is Deanna Simpson's sister, heard first that Ronnie Simpson had been killed.

"I called Carol Simpson, Deanna's sister-in-law, and she told me that he was reported as missing in action," Pat Allender remembers. "By this time, I had already heard that David Collins had been killed, and I had heard that several others had been wounded." Now, Pat was very concerned because she had not heard from her husband, who was in one of the gun crews in Charlie Battery. It was several days before she received a letter from him.

But when he called home Monday morning to talk to his parents, she did find out that he was not injured.

"I was canning green beans when I got a call from Donnie's mother, who wanted to talk to me. She said she was at the cleaner's, which was within walking distance, so I went there," Pat Allender remembers. "She said that Donnie had called, he was okay, and that he wanted to come home with Ronnie's body. At that time, we didn't even know if Ronnie was dead."

"Donnie Allender called home on Monday via the Red Cross and asked if he could escort Ronnie's body home," Deanna Simpson remembers. "That was the first time I knew for sure that Ronnie had been killed. The army said no, that they had trained body escorts for this."

"I was calling Mother and Dad, but they weren't home," Donnie Allender remembers, "so I talked to Sandy, my sister, who was fifteen at the time, and told her that I could escort Ronnie's body home but someone would have to go through the Red Cross with a request for me to do this.

"But it never did pan out, and three days later, I was transferred to another unit," he says.

A vine plant grows around a small American flag planted among the
military monuments outside the courthouse.

(PHOTO BY MARY ANN LYONS)

The Nelson County courthouse in Bardstown.
(PHOTO BY MARY ANN LYONS)

St. Joseph's Cathedral, Bardstown.
(PHOTO BY MARY ANN LYONS)

Hurst's drugstore is located in Bardstown's Courthouse Square.
(PHOTO BY MARY ANN LYONS)

Raymond Ford, first soldier from Bardstown to die in Vietnam. He was not in the Guard unit.

(PHOTO COURTESY OF MRS. BERTHA FORD)

Tom Raisor and wife, Mozena. He was outside starting generators when the attack began.

(PHOTO BY NEAL CORNETT)

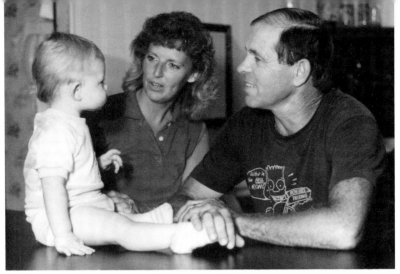

Ronnie and Libby Hibbs and grand-
child. He was burned by exploding
gunpowder as he left his gun, an
M-109 tracked 155 howitzer.

(PHOTO BY NEAL CORNETT)

Don Parrish holds flag that flew atop
Fire Base Tomahawk on the night of
the attack, June 19, 1969. Note the
shrapnel holes in the flag.

(PHOTO BY NEAL CORNETT)

Deanna Simpson
Sharpe, whose hus-
band, Ronnie Simpson,
was killed at Fire Base
Tomahawk.

(PHOTO BY NEAL CORNETT)

Charles Stone and wife, Betty.

(PHOTO BY NEAL CORNETT)

Jerry and Joy Janes. He was in Gun 1 and was wounded and burned.

(PHOTO BY NEAL CORNETT)

Wayne Collins in
Roung-Roung Valley.
*(PHOTO COURTESY OF
WAYNE COLLINS)*

Wayne Collins, critically
injured in the attack
on Tomahawk. Brother,
David, was killed.
(PHOTO BY JIM WILSON)

The former Mrs. Patsy
Collins, whose hus-
band, David, was killed
at Fire Base Tom-
ahawk. She married
Stanley Stone later and
is now divorced.
(PHOTO BY NEAL CORNETT)

Todd Collins, son of
David Collins, who
was killed at Fire Base
Tomahawk. The mem-
orial is one of two in
Courthouse Square
honoring those who
died in Vietnam.
*(PHOTO COURTESY OF
NEAL CORNETT)*

A sundial casts a shadow on the names of the Kentucky soldiers on the date they died, in this case June 19, 1969.

(PHOTOS BY JIM WILSON)

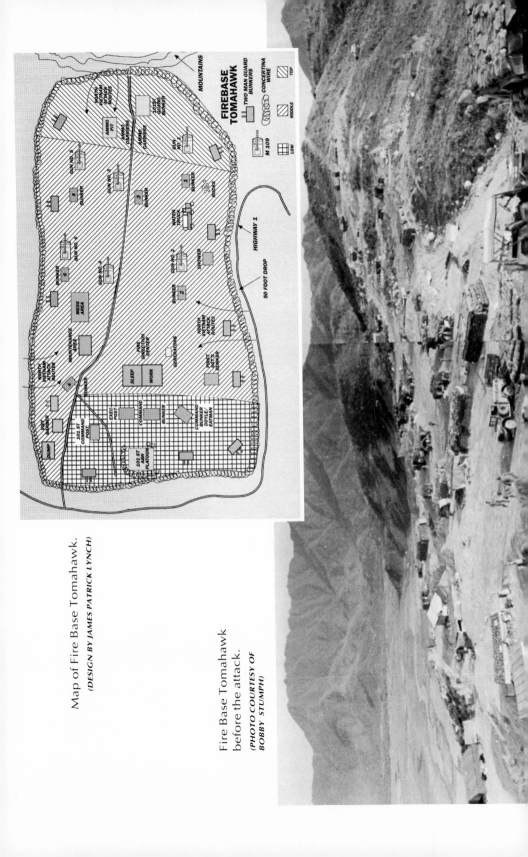

Map of Fire Base Tomahawk.
(DESIGN BY JAMES PATRICK LYNCH)

Fire Base Tomahawk
before the attack.
*(PHOTO COURTESY OF
BOBBY STUMPH)*

FIREBASE TOMAHAWK

MOUNTAINS

NORTH VIETNAM
RESUPPLY ROUTES

LEOST GUARD BUNKER

AMMO PIT

AMMO CARRIERS

GUN NO. 1

GUN NO. 5

5 BUNKER

3 BUNKER

1 BUNKER

ROCKS

WATER TRUCK

GUN NO. 6

GUN NO. 4

GUN NO. 3

6 BUNKER

MESS AREA

MAINTENANCE AREA

SHOWER

2 BUNKER

HIGHWAY 1

50 FOOT DROP

NORTH VIETNAM ATTACK ROUTES

FIRE DIRECTION CENTER

SLEEP   WORK

GENERATOR

CONCERTINA

FIRST SGT'S BUNKER

NORTH VIETNAM ROUTES

EXEC. POST

COMMAND POST

BUNKER

COMMAND BUNKER DOYLE/EATMAN

FIRST BARBER

DUMP

101ST COMMAND POST

101ST ABN PLATOON

TWO MAN GUARD BUNKERS

M 109

CONCERTINA WIRE

TOP

MIDDLE

LOW

FDC bunker before the attack.
(PHOTO COURTESY OF JERRY JANES)

(Left to right) Gary Bradbury, Jodie Haydon, Tom Raisor,
Jerry Janes, and Don Parrish.
(PHOTO COURTESY OF JERRY JANES)

Ronnie Simpson on
November 27, 1968,
standing atop Hill 88.
*(PHOTO COURTESY OF
DEANNA SIMPSON SHARPE)*

Ronnie Simpson on January 18,
1968, with three-legged dog,
Gertrude.

*(PHOTO COURTESY OF
DEANNA SIMPSON SHARPE)*

Gun 5 before the attack.

*(PHOTO COURTESY OF
JERRY JANES)*

Executive post bunker after the attack.

(PHOTO COURTESY OF JERRY JANES)

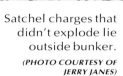

Satchel charges that didn't explode lie outside bunker.

(PHOTO COURTESY OF JERRY JANES)

Only debris remains from Jim Moore's gun. Door in foreground is from ammo carrier *(top)*.

(PHOTO COURTESY OF DON PARRISH)

Fire Base Tomahawk *(west to east)*. Two bodies lie in the foreground on the morning after the attack.
(PHOTO COURTESY OF DON PARRISH)

Gun 4 after the attack.
(PHOTO COURTESY OF BOBBY STUMPH)

Buck Harned on Hill 88 in spring 1969.

(PHOTO COURTESY OF JERRY JANES)

Barry Neal Thompson, who was killed on June 25, 1969.

(PHOTO COURTESY OF VENETA THOMPSON)

David Collins, who was killed in the attack. He went to get soup in the mess tent at 1:45 A.M. and saw North Vietnamese eating there.

(U.S. ARMY PHOTO)

Ronnie McIlvoy, who was in wire bunker and was killed just outside a doorway.

(U.S. ARMY PHOTO)

Jim Wray, who was transferred out of Battery C and was killed July 2, 1969.

(U.S. ARMY PHOTO)

Memorial at Tomahawk to those from Bardstown killed during June and July of 1969.
(PHOTO COURTESY OF JERRY JANES)

Twenty year reunion of those from Bardstown who survived the war.
(PHOTO COURTESY OF DON PARRISH)

"Everyone here knew who was on that hill and the entire town was greatly concerned," Mozena Raisor remembers. "I would say that if you brought up the Vietnam war at this time, you would get a very negative response, certainly not like the response would have been a few years ago."

"It seemed like the whole town went into mourning, it seemed like everyone was in a daze," Mary Collins says. "The wives that had not heard about their husbands were in total fear.

"Every minute seemed like a lifetime for those women as they waited to hear something, yet [were] afraid to pick up the phone, or answer a knock on the door," Mary adds.

"I could put myself in their position, because had I not heard about Wayne, I would be just as fearful as they were," Mary continues, "and I was very worried who the next one would be that had been killed.

"Remember, we were all close friends, we had all grown up together, all the guys were close, the wives had gotten very close, we were just like a family," Mary says.

Libby Hibbs was at home when she heard on the radio Monday morning that the unit had been attacked. "I didn't know what to do. Then friends began calling. They wanted information. I had none. Nothing." Then she called a close friend, Mary Collins, but no one answered. "I found out later that she had gone to her mother-in-law's house to be with them.

"Then I called Betty Stone, and she told me about David and Wayne," Libby says.

"Why don't you come over here and stay with me for a while," said Betty Stone, who was worried about her husband, Charles.

"I'll be there as soon as I can," Libby said. She took her baby to her mother, and she and Betty were together until the early morning hours, calling other wives, talking to friends, trying to find out if there were others who had been killed or wounded. Some could add a little information, others had not heard of the attack. As the hours passed that Monday, the town became aware of the tragedy atop Fire Base Tomahawk.

"Then we began to find out the names of the others who had

been killed or wounded," Libby says. "It was awful. Dreadful. I couldn't believe this was really happening to us.

"The mood of the town was one of sadness. Everyone was so depressed. It seemed like everyone was waiting for the next bit of bad news, for the name of the next one of our boys who had died or been wounded," she continues. "People would stop you on the street and ask you if you had any news, if there was anything they could do to help you."

It was almost two weeks before Libby learned of the fate of her husband, Ronnie. She never received any word from the army as to his status—was he wounded? missing? perhaps dead?

"My husband's uncle, A. V. Hibbs, called the Red Cross and told them about the attack, that my husband hadn't written or called, that we didn't know what had happened to him," Libby remembers. The Red Cross quickly located her husband in a hospital in Japan undergoing treatment for burns on his back and arms.

"His mom and dad, the whole family, came over to my house, and his uncle called Japan and we all got to talk to him," Libby remembers.

"I thought I was in heaven when I heard his voice," she says.

"How are you?" she asked.

"I'm fine, I'm not hurt bad," he answered. Then everyone talked to him for more than an hour.

Libby asked him why he hadn't written to her.

"I wrote you every day," he told her. He had. The letters all arrived a few days later in one big bundle.

Ronnie Hibbs never returned to Charlie Battery. When he left the hospital, his enlistment was just about up, so he was sent home.

Linda Blanford and her thirteen-month-old son lived with her parents in St. Francis, Kentucky, about eighteen miles from Bardstown. They didn't have a telephone, so there was no way to reach her and tell her about the attack on Charlie Battery. She heard two days later on television that the unit had been overrun, but she did not know if her husband, Louis T. Blanford, was safe. "I didn't know if he was alive, hurt, or if he was still there at the time, because he was scheduled to leave the unit on June 22, and maybe he left early," she remembers.

"His mother came over to my parents' house and told me he had called, that he had been wounded and that he was in the hospital," she relates. "She told me he'd call back as soon as he could, so I packed my clothes, took the baby, and stayed with his parents, waiting for him to call." About a week later, the telephone rang.

"How are you? Are you badly hurt?" she asked.

"I'm okay, I'm okay. I got hit in both legs, the back, and one shoulder, but I'm all right," he reassured his wife.

"How are you? How's the baby?" he wanted to know.

"We're both fine," she told him. "I'm so happy to hear your voice."

Then he gave her the names of those who had died, who were seriously wounded, who had suffered lesser wounds.

"He sounded pretty good to me, under the circumstances," Linda remembers.

"I was so worried," says his mother, Mrs. Twyman Blanford, "but I felt better after I talked to him. He sounded wonderful." She didn't know how badly he had been injured. "He just kept saying he would be all right," his mother says.

A few days after the attack, Betty McClure, whose husband was the battery commanding officer when the unit went overseas, and Nina Cundiff, wife of the battalion commander, Robert, talked to some of the wives and parents.

"We talked to Patsy Collins, we went to see her parents. We tried to talk to everyone," she remembers. "It was one of the hardest things I've ever had to do. It's very hard to extend condolences to someone whose husband has been killed, and your husband is still living."

By Tuesday, grief was everywhere. The people were numb, in shock.

"That was the saddest day that will ever hit Bardstown, or Nelson County," says Bill Jones, owner of a restaurant and a motel in Bardstown, and a resident of many years.

"I think at that moment, a whole lot of people wished the United States had never gotten into the war in Vietnam," Jones adds, "and I think a lot of 'em still feel that way today.

"The people here were pretty upset back then, and I think that's when the mood changed against the war," he continues. "And then, when the bodies started to come back, this was a pretty sad town," he says.

"I think it was a terrible war, but like I said before, when it started, I was all for it. But then it dragged on, and the way it was fought, I really did get bitter about it," he continues.

On Wednesday, June 25, Betty Stone and three other wives went to the funeral home to pay their respects to Sgt. Harold M. Brown, who had been killed on June 11. With Betty, whose husband, Charles, was in one of the gun crews that was attacked on Fire Base Tomahawk, were Patsy Collins, whose husband, David, had been killed; Mary Collins, whose husband, Wayne, had been critically wounded; and Patsy Moore, whose husband, Jim, had been burned over much of his body and later died.

David Collins, Ronnie Simpson, Ronnie McIlvoy, Jim Moore, Luther Chappel. This brought to eleven the number of young men from Bardstown, the local Guard unit, or close by who were killed in Vietnam. And the grief was far from over.

That same day, June 25, Barry Neal Thompson was killed by enemy gunfire near the Cambodian border. His mother, Veneta Thompson, never received a telegram from the army notifying her of her son's death, which is customary. Nor did she ever receive a telephone call. She found out about his death three days later, on Saturday, when an army sedan, by now an accustomed but not accepted sight along the streets and rural roads of this small farming community, showed up at her house at noon.

"A chaplain said simply that my son had died in action," Mrs. Thompson remembers, "and a few minutes later, he was gone.

"I was in shock, I was numb, very numb. There's no way to explain to you my grief," she adds. "You just had to experience it.

"It wasn't until much later that I found out through a telegram that the army sent me that he died of wounds to his head and neck near the Cambodian border," she continues.

She did, however, receive the following letter about three weeks after her son's death:

DEPARTMENT OF THE ARMY
COMPANY B. 1ST BATTALION, 28TH INFANTRY
(Lions of Cantigny)
APO San Francisco 96345

12 July 1969

Mr. and Mrs. Emmett B. Thompson
Route 2
Cox's Creek, Kentucky 40013

Dear Mr. and Mrs. Thompson:

I extend to you my most profound sympathy on the recent loss of your son, Specialist Fourth Class Barry N. Thompson, Company B, 1st Battalion, 28th Infantry. At approximately 2120 hours on 25 June 1969 at Delta Medical Hospital, your son died as a result of fragmentation wounds sustained in action against the enemy. He was fatally wounded earlier on this date while on an ambush patrol with his company.

News of your son's death comes as a great shock to all who knew him, and his loss will be felt deeply within this organization. I sincerely hope the knowledge that Barry was an exemplary soldier and died while serving his country will comfort you during your hours of sorrow.

Memorial services for Barry were not held at this time due to the tactical commitment of the unit. However, I can assure you that Memorial services will be held as soon as possible.

If we can be of any assistance, please do not hesitate to write. Once again, personally and for the officers and enlisted men of this command, please accept this letter as a symbol of our sympathy.

Sincerely yours,
FRANK S. DAVERSO
CPT, Infantry
Commanding

Captain Daverso was probably Thompson's commanding officer, because the unpleasant duty of informing next of kin of the loss of a loved one usually falls on the shoulders of the company commander.

"People around here were so upset, they were wandering around in a daze, wondering when it would all end, if there would be any more dead," Veneta Thompson adds.

"I've lived in this area all my life, I knew just about all those boys, and that period was by far the most traumatic that I have ever experienced," she says.

Betty Cook, the children's librarian at the public library in Bardstown, grew up with Barry Neal Thompson. "I went to his home to talk to his parents, to take some food. It was a very upsetting time," she remembers. "At the time of his death, he was going through a divorce.

"His parents were stunned," she adds. "I went to the funeral, and it was a sad time, a very sad time." Thompson and his wife, Janice, had a son, Barry Neal Thompson, Jr. He also had a daughter, Lynn Nichelle, age one, whose mother, Wanda Stumph, he planned to marry as soon as his divorce became final.

Later that day, Joy Brooks went to see Patsy Moore. Remembering that the Moores had two children, Joy took along some brownies. Patsy was getting a lot of calls, and people were stopping by, Joy remembers.

"I knew that Jimmy had died, I knew that the army officers had already been there, so I waited two or three days before I went to see her," Mozena Raisor remembers. "Jim's mom and dad were there.

"Patsy was hanging diapers on the clothesline when I saw her," Mozena says. "She told me that she told the men from Fort Knox that she wanted Tommy to come home with the body.

"She said that the two army officers told her, 'No, he cannot come home with the body because we have people with special training as body escorts who do this,'" she continues.

"She said she told 'em that if Tommy couldn't come home with his body, then just bury him over there and not to worry about it," Mozena Raisor adds.

"Patsy was just going through the motions that day, washing clothes and hanging 'em up methodically, sort of in a stupor," she remembers. Mozena's husband, Tom, was permitted to escort Jim Moore's body home.

Violet Chappel's husband, Luther, the first sergeant of Charlie Battery, shouldn't have been in Vietnam. His enlistment was due to expire in August of 1968, while the Guard battalion was in training at Fort Hood, Texas. But he wanted to stay with the men he had trained in Battery A, so he reenlisted for one year.

"I didn't want him to," says Violet, "but he was his own man.

"He said he could never look any of his men in the face if he did not go to Vietnam with them," she adds.

Chappel was a sergeant first class in Battery A when he went to Vietnam. A few months later, he received another stripe, was promoted to master sergeant, and was transferred to Charlie Battery.

"Don't worry about me, it's not even like war here," he continually wrote his wife and his two children, Charlene, nine, and Debra Kay, four.

The first time Violet Chappel heard of the attack on Charlie Battery was when two officers arrived at her mother's house, where she was temporarily living, and told her that her husband was missing in action. "I had chest pains, I was very nervous, so someone took me to the hospital, and they calmed me down," she remembers.

"While I was at the hospital, someone in his battery called and said that my husband had been killed. Later, the two officers came and told me at the hospital that my husband had been shot in the head and killed," she recalls.

"Although I'm married, and very happy, I think about it often, and every time I look at my grandchildren, I think of him," she adds.

"It was such a sudden blow, it put the whole community in a state of shock and sadness," Gus Wilson remembers. "I was mayor for twenty-four years, all through Vietnam, from start to finish, and, you know, we had quite a change in attitude along the way.

"The feeling of the people had already started changing so far as the war was concerned, and those who previously supported it were now beginning to turn away from the war in ever increasing numbers," Wilson adds. "Once it started changing, it changed quite a bit.

"Vietnam was like a bad business deal," the former mayor re-marks. "Write it off, wish it hadn't happened, and then make more money tomorrow.

"I think people were beginning to doubt the truth of what we were reading in the newspapers, seeing on television. And then when we had this sudden, tragic, and personal blow when our Guard unit was attacked, I think it changed the opinion of people a little faster," he observes.

"As for myself, I think I had quite a change in my feeling for the policy of the government, but I don't think I had a change in my feeling of patriotism," Wilson continues.

"I really feel like the leaders of our country just laughed at us," he says. "I think our leaders outright laughed at us, and that bothered me."

In the same issue of the *Kentucky Standard* that carried the news of the death of Barry Neal Thompson, the newspaper captured the mood of the people of Bardstown in their period of great agony. Its editorial of July 3, 1969, read:

> Sadness is spread over our community like a pall. Flags are half-mast as we mourn the loss of more of our valiant, courageous young men, young husbands, young fathers who have died heroes for their country, for our country, in an undeclared war against a com-munist aggressor in southeast Asia. They have paid the supreme sacrifice in Vietnam, as have other fallen heroes in other conflicts.
>
> On one side of the world, our fine specimens of young manhood fighting, dying, suffering wounds, giv-ing their all for a cause, the preservation of our free-dom and democratic way of life. On the other, except for spiraling inflation where the dollar is buying less, life goes on as in peacetime with no restrictions or hardships on the civilian population. We almost feel guilty that some are sacrificing all, and most of us nothing.
>
> Thoughtfully, we put ourselves in the place of

these grieved wives, sorrowing parents and families. They are accepting the pain, heartaches, magnanimously. If others of us were put to the test, could we bear the loss of these cherished loved ones, as heroically as they?

Surely we want to share one another's burdens, to comfort, to extend a helping hand.

But in our compassion, when we see this police action, half way around the world in a country torn by internal political strife, take such a heavy toll of our fine young men, can we help but question if our nation should be engaged in such a conflict, and [ask] ourselves repeatedly, when will it end?

Bill Medley, who was editor of the *Kentucky Standard* during the years 1980 through 1985, remembers that editorial and says that it caught the mood of Bardstown in its moment of grief.

The people, he says, were beginning to ask, "What in hell is going on over there? What are these boys from down the road being killed for?

"Many people lost faith in the war," he adds, "but few lost faith in their country.

"Vietnam was a shattering experience for people here, for people everywhere, and they will never forget it," he continues. "And for some families, their lives will forever be marked by that event.

"Back then, when someone suffered, it was more of a group experience, the deaths were mourned collectively," he explains.

Then the bodies began to come home. And the wounded.

"I just hope it'll be over so the ones over there can come home before they get killed, too," Dorothy Collins, the mother of David, who had been killed, and Wayne, who had been critically injured, said in an interview at that time.

"It isn't an individual affair when something like this happens," Charles Raisor, whose son, Tom, was injured slightly in the attack, said at that time. "It's a community affair. That Moore boy and Tommy were real close. They used to hunt and fish together."

Tom Raisor and Jim Moore had been very close friends since they were about fourteen. The same with Jim's brother, Joe.

"It was one foul day, and I was out there hunting for rabbits with my dogs. Joe and Jimmy were out there, too, and our dogs got together and took off," Tom Raisor says. "A lot of times, hounds will run together when they get out in the fields.

"I went over to get my dogs, and they were there, and we got to talking, and Jimmy said, 'You know, the next time you want to go hunting, if you'll call us, maybe we'll go somewhere together.'

"From that day on, the three of us were real good friends, and we'd go hunting or fishing almost every day, or at least [on] the weekend," Raisor says.

When the Guard unit was activated, both Jim and Joe were members of Battery C. "Why don't you join up?" Jimmy kept asking Raisor. "You're gonna get drafted."

"Aw, if I get drafted, the heck with it," Raisor answered. "You know, two years in the army will be better than spending six in the Guard."

Jimmy kept saying, "You better join!"

"Nah, I'll just wait," Tom kept telling him.

"You're gonna get drafted and wind up in Vietnam," Jimmy told him.

"Well, I'll take my chances," Raisor replied.

"But as the time kept getting closer and closer for me to be drafted," Tom explains, "I chickened out, so I went down to the Selective Service office and asked, 'Could you tell me where I stand so far as being called up?' "

They told him he was next.

"I walked out of that office and went straight to the armory and signed up," he says. "Luckily, there were still a few openings in the unit."

At that time, brothers did not have to go off to war. One could go, and one could remain behind. The Moore brothers decided that Jim would go, and Joe would remain behind to help with the trucking business. It was a difficult time for everyone back then.

"I was at the funeral home during what would be considered normal visiting hours. I had to be there to assist the family in any way that I could to help them get through the ordeal," Tom Raisor says.

"It was pretty rough on the whole family," Raisor remembers.

And it was extremely difficult on Raisor, whose mother didn't want him to go back to the hill and was very upset.

"There were a lot of families that came to the funeral home," Raisor says, "and each one wanted some assurance from me that a husband, son, brother, was okay.

"That was very tough on me," he adds.

Raisor was there for Jim Moore's funeral, but he left before the memorial service on July 4. All told, he was gone about two weeks.

Going back, he used the same words: "I'm a body escort . . ."

"I got back to Vietnam in July, but I never saw Tomahawk again because the unit had been moved to Phu Bai, where it was much safer." In October 1969, he came home for good.

Back in Bardstown, heavy hearts were everywhere as the bodies lay in flag-draped coffins in funeral parlors. "It seemed that everyone you talked to was either going to or coming from a funeral," Betty Stone remembers.

Then the wounded began to arrive.

A few days later, Jerry Janes was flown back to the United States and spent a little time in the hospital at Fort Knox. "I told him that when he arrived to call me and I'd come and meet him," Joy remembers.

"No," he told her, "I don't want you to meet me."

"So I went to see his parents, and his father told me that he'd pick me up around one P.M.," Joy says. "Well, it must have been around three P.M. when Mr. Janes picked me up. He said he went downtown to the drugstore and it must have taken him two hours to walk that short distance from his car because everyone wanted to stop and talk, to find out what was happening, to get the latest news." Two days later, on the Fourth of July, Joy went to Fort Knox and brought Jerry home.

"After he was home for a while, he began to worry me because for two or three weeks he kept saying, 'I don't feel right about being here, with the rest of the guys still over there.'

"It was as though he could not relax until they were all safe," she says.

"Lord help us all," she remembers thinking. "He's going to heal and head back over."

Buck Harned came back with Janes and was in the hospital at Fort Knox suffering from burns, wounds, and punctured eardrums. Then other wounded began to arrive there.

"It was the most tragic situation that ever happened here, by far," former Mayor Gus Wilson remembers. "The phone rang for four or five days, and it never stopped.

"Jim Sutherland, the county judge, and I got together and discussed what should be done. The editor of the newspaper, Elizabeth Spalding, was there. So was Bob Sallee, the police chief. Then we called in the Rev. George Lollis, a retired military chaplain and pastor of the First Christian Church of Bardstown," the former mayor recalls.

Together, they came up with an interdenominational service that was held in Bardstown High School on July 4.

"It's kind of hard to remember the memorial service, except that it was a very sad and depressing day," Mary Collins remembers. "Patsy and I went together. David's family, Patsy's family, we all sat together."

"It was the most traumatic experience in my life, but not just because of those in the Guard unit that had been killed, but for all the young men from Bardstown that lost their lives in Vietnam," she says.

The daughter of Ronnie and Deanna Simpson, Cheryl, was born June 29. Deanna left the hospital July 3 and went to the funeral home that night. Next day, she attended the memorial service.

"It was a very somber and very emotional day," she says. "My family was there, his family was there, just about everyone in town was there."

"I don't remember what went on. I was there. I remember being there, but I don't remember if we did anything or said anything, what they said, or anything else," Tom Raisor's wife says. "I just have this vague year of just being. I don't even remember if they had flags.

"It was really sad, and I think that's why I really don't remember anything about it," she adds.

Ruby Wray, whose husband, Jim, had been in Vietnam for several months, first heard about the attack on Fire Base Tomahawk a day, possibly two, after it occurred on June 19. She knew there were casualties. She heard it on television, and she was very concerned, very upset, because her husband had been in Charlie Battery but had been transferred out a few months earlier. So she knew a lot of the men in that Guard unit.

Ruby was at home in Louisville with her two daughters, Cindy, six, and Tracy, two. It was the Fourth of July, and she planned a quiet celebration. She knew the memorial service was under way in nearby Bardstown for those who had died on Fire Base Tomahawk. Her husband knew the men, had served with them.

But later that day, her sister called and asked her to bring her daughters and come over for hot dogs and hamburgers. A short time later, her brother came by and picked them up.

That evening, the army sedan stopped in front of her house. A neighbor told the men in the car no one was home.

"We can stay until ten P.M.," one of them said, and they waited.

"The neighbor didn't know where I was, but he did call an aunt who lived down the road, and she called me," Ruby remembers.

"My aunt said, 'There's an army chaplain here to see you,'" she adds.

"I knew right away what had happened, that my husband was dead," she says.

She hurried home, accompanied by her sister and brother. One of them called the family doctor.

The chaplain then told her that her husband had died July 2, 1969, as a result of injuries while on a military operation in Vietnam when supporting artillery impacted in his area. "I am sorry that he was killed by friendly fire," the chaplain added.

"I didn't know what friendly fire was," Ruby says.

"A short round from behind landed among the troops, and he was the only one killed in that mishap," said the chaplain in explaining the death of her husband, who was a gunner in the First Battalion, Fortieth Artillery.

"I just went to pieces," Ruby remembers. "The doctor had to give me a sedative."

The somber, touching memorial service in Bardstown began at nine A.M. with close to eight hundred wives, parents, family members, friends, and widows, some with children who would never see their father, others with children who would never see their father again, crowded into the school's auditorium. Others stood quietly outside.

Mayor Wilson read the names of those from the area who had been killed in Vietnam. Judge Sutherland noted, "None of us, yes, none of us, shall ever forget what they did there." There was an opening prayer, a closing prayer. "Taps" could be heard coming from the rear of the auditorium. A forty-nine-voice choir sang the "Battle Hymn of the Republic." A twenty-one–gun salute. Then it was over.

Betty Stone went to all the funeral homes, attended all the memorial services, spent time with all the women whose husbands had been killed or badly wounded.

She remembers just a little about the memorial service on July 4.

"The speakers, they said that you should be proud of those who had died, but that's hard to do when you grieve so. I don't think you know grief until you experience it, and I think they [the widows] definitely experienced grief.

"I remember Bobby Simpson being a pallbearer. I don't know why I remember that. I don't even know who went with me. I remember going to the funeral home to see Jim Moore. I remember Ronnie McIlvoy and Harold Brown and David Collins and Barry Neal Thompson," she says.

"And I remember the flags. I'd never seen so many flags in all my life. They had big flags up and down Main Street, large flags."

Libby Hibbs remembers going to the memorial service with Betty Stone, but that's about all. "I was totally in a trance. It was unreal. I cannot begin to explain my feelings," she says. "The grief was so great." She recalls thinking, "I'm gonna wake up, and this won't be so."

Betty McClure, whose husband, Tom, the commanding officer of Charlie Battery when it left for Vietnam, remembers the memorial service as a time of great sadness for the entire community.
"The whole town showed up," she says, "and people were standing
everywhere, inside the school, outside."

Ron Greenwell was there, taking pictures for the *Kentucky
Standard,* something that was very difficult for him to do. "I knew
most of the guys in Charlie Battery. I used to party with Jim Moore,"
he remembers.

"It was very solemn, very sad, and I just wanted to get away,
to get out of there," he says.

He remembers, too, photographing the funeral of Raymond
Ford, the first young man from Bardstown to get killed in Vietnam.
"That was the first time that Vietnam touched Bardstown," recalls
Greenwell.

"I don't remember there being a lot of people at Ford's funeral, though, just family and friends," he says. "Of course, he was
the first to die, and at that time no one was thinking there would be
so many more," adds Greenwell, who was drafted and spent a year in
Vietnam with the Ninth Infantry Division.

John Laurence, a correspondent for the CBS television news
who had covered the fighting in Vietnam, also covered the memorial
service.

One evening at dinner, he told the mayor: "The government
is not shooting straight with the people of the United States,
and you are going to find this out, and you are not going to be as
patriotic.

"We can't win this thing. It's useless. You people are being
fooled, and you don't know it," Laurence told the mayor.

"I'll never forget the gist of this conversation," Mayor Wilson says.

About two weeks after the attack on Fire Base Tomahawk,
Wayne Collins called his wife, Mary, from a military hospital
in Japan.

"It was about two o'clock in the morning. My dad answered
the phone, then came and told me, 'Mary, Wayne's on the phone.'

"For a second, I just froze, I was so excited. When I heard

his voice, I just couldn't believe it. I cried and cried," she remembers.

"Then I began to talk, but you had to say 'over' all the time, so it was awkward to express my feelings," she says.

"How are you and my little baby?" Wayne asked.

"We're doing well, everything is fine," she said between sobs, tears running down her cheeks.

"Everyone is doing well. When are you coming home?" Mary wanted to know.

"I'll be home in a few weeks," he told her.

"He was very worried about his parents," she remembers, "and I told him that they were holding up."

Wayne Collins remained in the hospital in Japan for three weeks, then was transferred to Walter Reed Army Hospital in Washington, D.C. As soon as she could, Mary and her son went to visit him.

"I would say without doubt that the most emotional moment in my life occurred when I was walking around the hospital looking for him, but he saw me first," Mary remembers. "He had never seen the baby, who was about six months old at the time. I will never forget the look on his face when he walked up and looked at me, then looked at his son, and said, 'There's my little buddy.'

"I cried and cried," she says.

She stayed in Washington for three days. By this time, Wayne was up and walking, so they had three wonderful days together. Two weeks later, he was released and went home.

———

Gloom and uncertainty seemed to hang over Bardstown for the next few months. How much grief can a very small town endure?

"The town was on edge until the unit was taken off the hill, then everyone began to relax just a little," Mozena Raisor says. "Later, when the men began to come home, then everyone began to feel so much better.

"Remember, we had all put our dreams, our futures on hold, some of us forever," she adds.

That wonderful moment came on October 11, 1969.

There were hundreds of gallons of coffee, doughnuts by the hundreds of dozens, cameras, picnic baskets, camp chairs, blankets, and baby strollers. More than three thousand men, women, children, mothers, wives, sweethearts, gathered at Shewmaker Air National Guard Base in Louisville to welcome home the 386 men in the Second Battalion, 138th Artillery, returning from a year in Vietnam. A chill wind bit through the throng. It could have snowed. It would have made no difference. Nothing could dampen the excitement, the happiness of the crowd.

Signs were everywhere. "Here I am, Daddy." "I'm Over Here, Johnny." "Here We Are." There was even a sign that read, "Hurray for the Army."

The talk was not of war. Instead, people were asking, "Can the Mets' pitching stop the Orioles?" "Will he remember me?" "He hasn't seen his son."

They began arriving early in the evening the night before the two planes were scheduled to land. By midnight the air base was jammed. It was like the state fair, the Fourth of July, and Christmas jammed into one giant celebration. At 3:30 A.M. they learned that the first jet would touch down in two hours with 164 men aboard, most of them from Battery A. At 5:42 A.M. the big commercial jet landed and the throng began to surge forward, some people crossing the yellow line that they were supposed to remain behind. An officer on a loudspeaker urged them backward, and they complied. American flags popped up everywhere, small ones clutched in the hands of children, large ones proudly held high by their parents. The first to step off the plane was the commanding officer of the artillery unit, Lt. Col. Robert Cundiff of Hodgenville, Kentucky. He spotted his wife. She saw him and broke from the crowd, crossing the yellow line, and ran toward him, and the crowd followed. Gone was the military formation that had been planned. Protocol went out the door. It was laughter and tears, wives and babies. Pandemonium reigned for more than an hour. Then calm returned as loved ones waited for the second plane to land, bringing the sixty-five men still in Charlie Battery back to Bardstown and their loved ones. An army band played "My Old Kentucky Home."

The second plane landed, the men got off, the crowd raced toward them, and pandemonium once again was the order of the day.

"I remember when Tom got off the plane," Betty McClure says. "I was so glad to see him. I cried. My family was there. His family was there. The kids were there. I also remember how bad he looked, but I was just so happy to see him." The men were given a few days to spend with their families, then told to report to Fort Knox the following Monday for processing out of the service.

"By the time I got back to Bardstown, a lot of things had settled down," Tom McClure says. "The town had had a huge memorial service at the high school. Then there was a big welcoming home for us, part of which was solemn in memory of those who hadn't come home. But our people were there, and they welcomed us. Our community did support us.

"But overall, the people were somewhat disenchanted with it all, with the fighting," he adds. "They didn't talk about it much because we were back. They respected our feelings."

Despite the great joy in Bardstown and the small communities close by, it was extremely difficult for the people to pick up the pieces and go on with their lives, to regain the happiness they had before the call-up of the Guard unit. Some would never be able to put it together again. And the dying wasn't over.

Army Sgt. Paul Johnson was killed August 4, 1970. He was from nearby New Haven. Sgt. Nicholas Gerald Johnson was killed August 13, 1970. He, too, was from New Haven. SP4 Charles David St. Claire, from nearby Cox's Creek, was killed on January 16, 1971.

Before the killing would come to an end, one more body would come home to Bardstown, that of Air Force Capt. James J. Crawford, who was killed February 3, 1972. His was the last name on one of two monuments in Courthouse Square dedicated to those who lost their lives in the war.

The Crawfords had a daughter, Ellen, who is now in college. She never saw her father.

"My daughter is very bitter that she didn't get to know her

dad," Rebecca Crawford says, "but I don't know that she was bitter against the war.

"This important part of her life is missing," James Crawford's widow continues. "People would say to her, 'I know how you feel,' and she'd say, 'No, you don't.'

"I don't know what she felt, and how she felt about [not having a father,] but we've been fortunate to have been able to go on and have a life, and I think we're close, in a way," Rebecca Crawford adds. "We're closer in a way that maybe we wouldn't have been had her father lived."

Flying was her husband's life when they met. It was his life during their marriage. It was his life when his plane crashed in the jungle while returning to Udorn Air Force Base in Thailand after a mission.

"He wanted to fight in the war," Rebecca Crawford says of her husband. "He said that he hoped he could help make peace in the world.

"I felt disillusioned that a lot of times I don't think we knew what was really going on," she says of the fighting is Asia.

Her husband often told her about the phone call she might get, or the little blue air force car that might show up at her home, the one that brought the two officers, just as the army sedan had done so often in Bardstown over the past few years.

Rebecca Crawford was visiting an aunt and uncle in Indiana when she learned of her husband's death. When the two air force officers arrived at her home in Bardstown, no one was there. Her mother, who also lived there, was at work at Ice's Produce. A neighbor saw the two officers, walked over, and asked, "Can I help you all?"

"We're looking for Mrs. Rebecca Crawford," one of them replied.

"She's not at home. Can I take a message?"

"No."

The neighbor, who ran a funeral home, pretty much guessed what the situation was as soon as he saw the air force sedan and the two officers.

"He knew that my mother was at work, so he went down and got her and brought her home," Rebecca says.

"Why are you here?" her mother asked.

"Well, we can't say," Her mother knew why they were there, too. That's part of life in the military. One of the officers called Fort Knox and got permission to drive to Indiana, and the three of them left.

"For some reason, my aunt looked out the window and said, " 'Well, here comes your mother and some friends of yours,' " Rebecca recalls.

"Well, they're not friends of mine," she remembers saying. "But as soon as I saw them," she continues, "I knew what it was.

"Then they came in, and the guy was so cold, he was really cold. He just read sort of an obituary, and that was it," she relates. "It was just like he pushed a button, and he started reciting it a second time."

"I can't believe this," she remembers saying.

"My father died when I was young, and I was never treated to any special privileges because I didn't have a father. That's just the way life was dealt. I think that Ellen has definitely picked that up—that you don't get any special privileges just because you don't have a father," Rebecca adds.

"Life goes on in the big city, and I know during that time I said this was something that I didn't have any part of—the fact of her father dying," she explains. "I mean, it wasn't like a divorce. It wasn't like a separation or anything of that sort. This was totally out of my hands. This was just the way it was dealt. We had to make the most of it."

The war, she says, "was just devastating, but Bardstown hung together over the years and the people continued to support each other.

"If somebody needs help, there's always somebody here to give it. We have a lot of transient people that come in and go out. We get kids at school today that have no relatives here," says Rebecca, a school nurse. "We can't figure out why they're here, or how they got here.

"Sometimes we feel like there's a sign out here on the edge of town—'Come Here, and We'll Take Care of You,'" she continues.

As for the death of Captain Crawford, she says: "I don't think all bad came from my husband being killed in the war. There had to be a reason for it all. But I think there's been good. If nothing else, just the concern and the compassion, just being there for each other has been good.

"The war is always here," she adds, touching the back of her head, "and it will always be there, I'm sure."

Several years ago Rebecca Crawford and her daughter went to Washington, D.C., to visit the Vietnam Veterans Memorial. Before she went, she felt the memorial was a big waste of money, she says. "I thought, 'Well, we'll go there, see the wall, and that will be it.' Well, the feeling that was there in the area of the wall, was just . . . I totally lost all control. My daughter, Ellen, who was twelve at the time, had to take care of me the rest of the day.

"I want her to feel that her daddy was doing a good job. I mean, doing some good. You know, if [the war] was all bad, then what was her daddy doing there? She doesn't have much to grasp as far as what he was and what he was like," she says. "I think that it was an honor for him to be a pilot."

■

The surprise attack on Fire Base Tomahawk took one last life in Bardstown. Dorothy Collins, mother of David and Wayne, was found in her home, a shotgun by her side, a few weeks after Charlie Battery came home from the war.

■

The war in Vietnam lasted ten years, from 1965 until 1975. By 1973, most American troops were gone from the distant land that even in wartime was a beautiful country. Saigon fell on April 30, 1975. By that time, 58,132 Americans had lost their lives, 61,609 had been wounded, and 2,436 were reported to be missing in action.

"I've never had a really clear-cut opinion as to exactly what we were about there [in Vietnam]. It includes such things as the war was a boost to this nation's economy, we were there to stop the spread of communism, and we were there at the whim of the slow learners in Washington—both houses of Congress, I'm speaking of—for whatever their reasons were at the time," Don Parrish says.

"I'm really torn on that subject," he adds, "but I am probably one of the last, if not the last, member of this community that still states that we had a purpose there.

"I think the effort to win was entangled in politics in Washington. I think there was, at various times, a sincere effort made to win the thing," Parrish continues, "but unfortunately, I believe the economy had as much bearing on it as anything else. In wartime, this nation has less unemployment and a stronger economy.

"On the day that Saigon fell, I got a real empty feeling with that. It really took a lot of the value out of the sacrifice that so many guys had made," Parrish explains.

"That really took a lot of the wind out of the sails, and I had lots of problems with it. I thought about it a whole lot. Of course, we knew it was happening, it was gonna happen, and it did happen, but I still couldn't believe it."

On one of the marble monuments in the center of town close to the courthouse are these words:

"In Memory Dedicated to These Men Who Gave Their Lives in Vietnam 1969 for the Preservation of Freedom."

"As it turned out, we don't know," says Kent Bischoff. "I hope they didn't die for nothing, but it almost looked like that with the fall of Saigon in 1975."

"It was the most traumatic period in the history of our town," remembers historian Dixie Hibbs. "The acceptance of the war here was so much greater at the beginning than it was at the end. Nevertheless, I'm glad our boys went—to Vietnam, not to Canada."

Postscript

I f you like history, enjoy a walk in the past, you'll like Bardstown. This small country town has changed very little since that fateful day of June 19, 1969. People here still live in the great, old homes that their parents occupied. They still worship in the same beautiful churches as did their grandparents.

"It's an old town," says the former mayor, Gus Wilson. "There are statutes for everything. Sometimes it gets confusing. You can't change the exterior of your house, or the exterior of any other building, without going through the Bardstown Historic Zoning Commission.

"If you want to add a traffic light on one of the town's two major thoroughfares, Stephen Foster Highway, which runs east and west, or Third Street, which runs north and south, then you have to go through the Kentucky State Highway Commission," the former mayor explains, "because those two thoroughfares are controlled by the state.

"I think our little town will grow," Wilson says. "I just hope it doesn't grow too fast.

"If you sit still, though, you go backward," he adds, "and I don't think the majority of our people want us to go backward."

Bardstown, over the years, has grown, but slowly. Back in 1965, the population was 5,273. By 1970, it had grown to 6,040.

The population today is a little more than 8,000, according to the present mayor, Chuck Brauch.

"There are so many people," Joy Janes says. "I used to go downtown, and I'd know everyone. In 1969, everyone you'd see was a native, had grown up here. I just hope it doesn't get much bigger, for my sake, for my children's sake."

Back in the mid-1960s, when the war was new, a lot of young people moved away after they had graduated from high school, mostly because there weren't jobs, partly because of the war. But that's changed now. New industry has moved in. There are more jobs. Japanese immigrants have arrived, bringing with them new dollars and employment.

"When I came here in 1966, it was a good town to live in," says Mayor Brauch. "Today, it's better. There are more opportunities for [people] to stay here and work."

"Irregardless of why you left, be it a disagreement with your parents [over the war], jobs, looking for freedom, excitement, when it comes right down to it, the atmosphere, the warmth and sincerity, tend to draw people back," says Bobbie Brown, who runs her family's motel on the edge of town. "Especially when you're trying to raise a family."

Families here are large. Ten children are not uncommon. "We had to creep in at night when nobody saw us because we only had four kids," Mayor Brauch says facetiously.

Although Bardstown takes great pride in the fact that it is the bourbon capital of the world—in production, not consumption—tourism is considered the major industry here, and just about everyone here has a hand in it, in one way or another. Each tourist dollar turns over seven times before it leaves the area.

There are problems here, too. There are burglaries. You lock your doors now, something you didn't need to do in years past. There are drugs. And alcohol.

"There was always a drinking problem here," says Dixie Hibbs, the historian and a member of the city council. "I guess that's because of the distilleries, to some extent. But are we bad because we make whiskey? Are we bad because we drink it? No.

"But we do condone immoderation," she says. "We now publish the names of those caught driving under the influence. As a result, the fatality rate is going down.

"Nevertheless, alcohol is a bad problem here now. I consider it our biggest problem," she adds.

Mayor Brauch, discussing the use of alcohol by young people here, says, "Drinking is a problem. I think that's one of our big problems. We've tried to be tough on establishments that sell to minors."

"Even though Bardstown is not without problems," Mrs. Hibbs says, "it's still a nice place to live. We're still getting people back who left during the war because they are finding Bardstown a very nice place to raise a family.

"You could be successful in a big city, but not be able to walk down the street," she adds. "You can walk down the street here."

"Traffic is a problem, too," the mayor adds, "but that's because of all the new homes being built around town. We are concerned about our traffic. If you have to wait for a traffic light, that's a traffic jam."

They're working on a bypass that city planners hope will take away a lot of the traffic on the town's narrow streets, certainly the big trucks.

Empty stores in the downtown area, a product of new shopping malls that have opened a few miles away, are a problem. A group of concerned residents are working to resolve this.

"It concerns me that so many stores on Main Street are becoming vacant," remarks Ben Guthrie, who was born here in 1918.

"At night, when I drive through town around nine o'clock, well, in the old days, fifteen or twenty years ago, there used to be people on the streets, hanging around, loafing, talking, but now, the sidewalks, they just seem to roll 'em up," Guthrie says. "That's what I notice more than anything else."

Hurst's Drugstore is still here, still a gathering place in the morning, and after school, but television has killed the evening crowd. Still, the "Welcome" sign is always out, particularly for children, who seem to have the run of the place. Quite a few years ago, Hurst had a close working relationship with Walgreen's, the big, powerful, influential firm in Chicago. Those ties are gone now, but Hurst remembers them fondly. "Nowadays, it's hard to talk to a doctor," Hurst says. "If you call his office and say, 'This is Bobby Hurst . . . ,' you get his secretary, or his office manager, or somebody else. But when I call and say, 'This is Bobby Walgreen . . . ,' you'd be surprised how quickly I get through."

There were no blacks in Battery C when the unit left for Vietnam, although a few transferred in after it got there.

Bardstown does have a black population, about sixteen or seventeen percent. "We've got blacks here who are a problem," says Don Parrish, who was a member of the city council for several years, "but we've got a lot more whites who are bigger problems."

"Bardstown is a nice place to live," agrees Brenda Ford, whose brother, Raymond, a black, was the first person from Bardstown to die in Vietnam. "It's the place that I came back to. I was married and my husband was an officer in the army, and when we divorced, I thought that Bardstown would be the ideal place to come back to and raise my daughter as a single parent. And I have never regretted it."

The people here have not forgotten those who died in Vietnam. The American Legion's Old Kentucky Home Post 121 remembers those who answered the call, from all wars.

"Even though people became very disenchanted with Vietnam, this is still a pretty patriotic town," former Mayor Wilson feels.

"I volunteered and spent five years in the army in World War II, because I thought this is what you're supposed to do," the former mayor says. "I got a little bit upset with some of our younger generation, including one of my own sons, who didn't quite have that feeling. He went, but he didn't feel like I did about it."

———

As battles in wartime go, the attack on Fire Base Tomahawk by the North Vietnamese was not a great one, in either breadth or scope. It had no effect on the outcome of the war, which many people throughout the United States felt we had already lost. It was not a turning point. But the attack on Battery C the night of June 19, 1969, carved a tiny niche in the pages of history for Bardstown and the National Guard unit, and whenever historians research that ten-year war, Battery C and this very small town will be there for all to see. Like it or not, Bardstown is a small part of the history of that war.

Battery C had several months of complacency, of false security, before the men heard that first shot fired in anger, took their first casualty. If you were to ask each man who was there that night, he would, in all probability, say that an attack of this nature was inevitable, given the questionable position in which the artillery battery was placed: about ninety men and six big guns dug in on moderately high ground with hills around them that were much higher. And a perimeter far too large to protect. Add to this the fact that very few of the men carried their weapons with them at all times, and you have the setting for just what happened—a devastating surprise attack.

And then there was the much-disliked infusion program, under which half or more of the men in the battery were transferred out and regular army men moved in, causing a morale problem.

"I absolutely did not like that program. It destroyed team spirit and teamwork," says Brig. Gen. Thomas R. Ice, now assistant commander of the Thirty-fifth Infantry Division, which is made up of units from five states, one of which is Kentucky.

"This unit had trained together for a year, and to move those people elsewhere was not the most intelligent thing to do, in my opinion," says Ice, who on the night of the attack was a young officer back in the Fire Direction Center at Gia Lai, about eight to ten miles west of Phu Bai and adjacent to Camp Eagle and the 101st Airborne.

"Some people look at it this way: if infusion had not taken place, the grief back home would have been much worse," Ice says.

"I like to look at it in another way: if the full complement of Bardstown men had remained there, there may never have been an attack," he adds.

"The reason for the infusion was not because the men were

all from one town," he explains. "The army realized that after we all put in our one year, we would all be gone, that there would be a unit there on paper, and equipment, but no men. The closeness of our people in our small town was only an afterthought."

"When all of our guys were together, when we went on the perimeter at night, you knew that you could lay down and sleep because they'd be awake," says Charles Stone, who was on the hill the night of the attack. "When they started infusing these other guys, these regular army guys, well, you'd get up next morning, and they'd be in their guard bunkers asleep."

Many of the men who infused into Battery C did not have skills at the high level required to move into a gun crew. They needed to be retrained, reoriented, but there were so many new faces in the unit, there was no time to do this.

An after-action report dated July 7, 1969, states that thirty-seven men in the artillery battery were taken off the hill wounded, and that thirteen men in the airborne infantry platoon were wounded and evacuated. The report further said that four men in the airborne platoon died that night, in addition to those in Battery C.

———

There are two monuments in Courthouse Square, one dedicated to those young men from Bardstown and nearby communities who died during the war, the other dedicated to the seven men killed between June 11 and July 2, 1969, who had been in Battery C or who had recently transferred out. This includes the names of the four who died the night of June 19, and one who died a few days later from burns suffered that night. When a tragedy of this magnitude touches a very small town, it will draw the media, television and print, from far and wide. Bardstown was on the nightly news programs immediately. Camera crews and reporters were everywhere, seeking out widows, wives, parents, friends; trampling on their sensitivities; prying; asking delicate questions in an indelicate manner; misquoting; and in general leaving a bad impression of the media in the minds of many residents here. Over the years, reporters would drift in, ask a few questions, draw conclusions for which there was little basis, then depart. The best way to handle this situation, many of the residents decided, was simply not talk to the media. Some residents did talk to the press, but many did not. Of those who I talked to, one declined politely to go into any detail, one was rude, and the members of one family said they would rather not discuss the matter.

Over the weekend of August 11–13, 1989, when the artillerymen held their twentieth reunion, the media again descended on Bardstown. "Sunday Morning" with Charles Kuralt was there, filming the memorial service, talking to survivors and their families. Just about everyone who participated agreed that it was very tastefully done by CBS.

"The twentieth reunion wasn't a rehashing of the war," remembers Jerry Janes. "It was a 'How you doing?' 'How's the family?' 'How many kids you got?' type of gathering."

Charles Harbin, a former commander of Battery C, remembers the reunion. "It was a good time, a blessing to see how good everyone looked, how strong they were," he says. "I saw vitality in everyone. These were hometown people, never into the drug culture, strong spiritually, morally, and physically." There are a lot of veterans of Vietnam here, men who were drafted, who enlisted because they didn't want to be drafted or who simply felt it was the right thing to do. Many were wounded. Air force Col. James E. Bean was a prisoner of war for five years. We are talking about men who did not have hot meals three times a day, showers, bunks on which to sleep; some had sheets, a few had pillows. We're talking about men who had to root out the enemy with hand grenades and bayonets from their jungle strongholds. We're talking about men who, night after night, fought battles far greater than that at Fire Base Tomahawk. Over the years, a certain amount of resentment has developed on their part toward the media attention the artillery battery has generated. The resentment, however, is not directed toward individuals in Battery C. This is for all of them, for Raymond Ford, for William Russell Taylor, for Ron Greenwell, for everyone here whom the war in Vietnam touched, not just for those in Battery C.

It wasn't just the men in Battery C who feared Fire Base

Tomahawk, who felt that it was a bad hill, a bad position to place any unit, let alone an artillery outfit with minimum protection.

Airborne Capt. John Anderson first saw Tomahawk in late January of 1969. He went there to meet the men of a battery of 105 howitzers who would be firing in support of a battalion of infantry of the 101st Airborne Division. Anderson, an artillery officer, would be the liaison between the two units, so he wanted to talk to the battery commander about what kind of weather to expect, whether mud and water would create a problem for the howitzers, how much contact they had with the enemy, how good the intelligence was. But once he got up to the fire base and got his first look at the hill, about all he could think of was the very bad location.

"This is a terrible place to be," Anderson remembers thinking. "We will actually have people firing down on us from good cover and concealment. Too many people can bring direct fire on us from pretty dense terrain."

"I didn't like it at all," he says. "That was my first visit to the fire base, and I was not happy about it." Three days before he got there, monsoon rains had waterlogged sandbags and ammunition boxes filled with sand, and their great weight brought down the roof of a bunker, killing one man. The men were still talking about that when Anderson got there, so he couldn't wait to get off the hill.

A few months later, he became a battery commander, and a short time after that, his unit was assigned to Fire Base Tomahawk.

"I wasn't too happy about that," he says. "I'd been there before." He was only there three days, though, then moved elsewhere.

Most of the men in Battery C still live around here. The former Patsy Collins and Deanna Simpson are still close friends. "Over the years, I kept telling Deanna how smart she was to never marry again," Patsy says. "She always laughed when I told her that.

"But the divorce rate in Bardstown is very high," Patsy adds.

The former Mrs. Collins, whose husband, David, was killed during the attack on Fire Base Tomahawk, is a substitute teacher here, a teacher's aide at times, and the official timer at basketball games. Her son, Todd, was born two months before the death of his father. "David and I talked about my getting pregnant, having a baby, before he left for Vietnam. We talked about the possibility of him not coming back, and if this happened, then there would be a child. I wanted this," she says. Her son, Todd, a few years ago married Cheryl Moore, the daughter of Jim and Patsy Moore. Jim Moore died as a result of burns he received during the fighting. His wife has since remarried.

In December of 1970, Patsy Collins married Stanley Stone, who was also on the fire base when it was attacked, and they had three children. They have been divorced for more than ten years. Stanley Stone still lives here.

"I don't think any good came out of the war," the former Mrs. Collins says. "We lost a lot of young men over there, for no reason.

"I think the town still feels a lot of pain, certainly the older people. A lot of the younger people don't remember. But everywhere you go, there's something to remind you of it. You run into somebody you knew then, you see a face, there's always something to remind you. It just won't go away," she says.

"I look back and can't believe that it's been almost twenty-five years since David was killed," she continues. "Even so, I remember it every day.

"Over the years, I've seen David many times, always in crowds, always from the rear," Patsy says. "He'll always be with me, I'll never forget him."

Her brother, Charles Dickerson, who was in Vietnam but not in the Guard unit, was critically injured when shrapnel cut a vein in his throat. Mrs. Collins's husband was killed, her brother-in-law was seriously wounded and almost lost a leg, her brother almost bled to death, and her mother-in-law took her own life, all because of the war.

"Will this happen again? Will they call up our sons? I think about it a whole lot, with so much war going on. Is it going to be their turn?" she wonders.

———

Mary and Wayne Collins still live here. They both work. Their children are grown.

"The day of looking out that window and seeing that soldier come to my door always comes back," she says. "I won't forget it.

"When Wayne was in the hospital at Da Nang, they came very close to amputating his very badly wounded leg, but at the last minute, the doctor decided against it. Instead, they removed a vein from the bad leg and replaced it with one from the good leg," she adds.

"I'd give anything in the world to know who the doctor was, so we could thank him," Mary says. "I don't know how many times I've thought about him and said thank you."

Wayne Collins is considered by the Veterans Administration to be sixty-five percent disabled, and it was a year before he could return to work.

Years later, the Collinses and their children visited the Vietnam Veterans Memorial in Washington, D.C. "We just stood there, looked at all those names, and I thought, 'My God! What did we do?' They were all in their twenties. They never had a chance," Mary remembers.

The former Deanna Simpson, whose husband, Ronnie, died in the attack on Fire Base Tomahawk, still works for the same law firm that she did more than twenty-five years ago. She's married now, to a police officer, Dennis Sharpe, whom she had known for several years. Her daughter, Cheryl, is also married.

"I've seen second marriages fail because of young children, so I didn't think there was anything wrong with waiting until my daughter grew up and got married," she explains.

"I saw a lot of friends that I went to school with come into the law office where I work to get their first and second divorces," she adds, "and I just didn't want anything like that to happen to me.

"When I was young, I just wanted to get a good job and a good husband, have a home and family, not necessarily in that order, but the war took it all away.

"But I have it now," she adds.

"After Ronnie was killed, I was really scared, as I am sure

the others who lost their husbands were. Having the total responsibility for raising a child was overwhelming to me. Reporters would come to town and ask me for an interview. I just didn't want to talk about it. I just wanted to get on with my life, and talking about it just brought those feelings back like it happened yesterday.

"In most of the articles, the names of the men who were killed from Bardstown were mentioned. After my husband's name, there was always the statement that I was still unmarried. That hurt, because I felt I knew what the writer was insinuating —that perhaps there was something wrong with my thinking because I didn't remarry quickly. I didn't like that. I have the right to remain single or remarry without coming under the scrutiny of others.

"In 1982, an article in the Louisville *Courier-Journal* said, 'Deanna Simpson is living in the past. . . .' The article stated that I had kept my husband's car and built a two-car garage around it as a memorial to him. When I read that, I was devastated. I felt like the person or persons who gave that information to the reporter were after me, or had something against me. I guess those who gave that information didn't know what a two-car garage looked like, because I didn't build it. It was already there. I parked my husband's car in it, as one normally would if they had a garage.

"Everyone was hurt enough from what happened over there, and for someone from your own hometown to intentionally say something to a reporter that he or she knew would hurt a lot of people who had already been through enough was cruel and thoughtless."

The fall of Saigon was agonizing for the men of Battery C.

"I just couldn't see us getting up and leaving everything over there, just giving it over [to the enemy]," says Charles Stone, who, with his wife, Betty, still lives in Bardstown.

Stone, who was wounded when an RPG exploded inside his

Gun 4, says, "I just couldn't believe that we'd ever do that. You know, when you have people bringing in supplies on elephants, and we have helicopters, sophisticated weapons, things like that, we should have walked all over them."

Jerry Janes, who was also wounded during the attack, and his wife, Joy, and their six children live on a quiet, tree-lined street in a house that was built more than eighty years ago. He's been a member of the city council for twelve years. He's coached basketball; is a member of the Nelson County Planning and Zoning Commission, the chamber of commerce, and the finance committee of St. Joseph's Cathedral; and belongs to the Knights of Columbus.

As for Vietnam, he has this to say: "At the time, I thought this was a legitimate situation, and that we were where we were supposed to be. Since then, my opinion has changed. Once you saw the amount of military equipment and the great number of soldiers we had there, you realized that this was just a big game. There's no way we should have lost. What we lost were a lot of lives, and for what? If someone in government can tell me what we accomplished there, I wish they would tell me, because I don't think we accomplished a damn thing."

"It was Holy Thursday when the Guard unit was called to active duty," Joy Janes remembers, "and every Holy Thursday it all comes back, the heartbreak, the disappointment."

Don Parrish, just like Jerry Janes, has always had a keen interest in local politics, in civic affairs. He served fourteen years on the city council, lost his seat a few years ago, and hopes to serve again. Parrish, who was in the Fire Direction Center the night of the attack, is on the city and county planning commission and the historic zoning commission for Bardstown, and is chairman of the downtown council that is trying to revitalize Bardstown's central business district. He is married, has two daughters, and owns a firm that manufactures concrete blocks. One of his possessions that he is proudest of is the flag that flew on top of Fire Base Tomahawk the night of the attack.

"We have a wall in Washington that we've been to with fifty-eight thousand names on it. We killed over five million people in that country. The bottom line is, we need to avoid war at all cost. War is stupid," Parrish adds.

━━━━

Bobby Stumph, who was injured during the attack, and his wife, Lorraine, farm about 150 acres a few miles from Bardstown. After his return from Vietnam, he went back to work at the Ford tractor division just outside Bardstown; then he went into business for himself repairing farm machinery until he had an accident on his farm far more harrowing than anything that happened to him in Vietnam. In October of 1989, he was discing a small garden behind his house when the disc caught an electrical guide wire, a transformer fell on his tractor, and he fell off and under the disc.

"I had a small beauty shop here at the time, and the lights were going crazy, so I went out to see why," Lorraine remembers. "I saw him under the disc, and the tractor was moving, slowly, because it was in second gear.

"I tried to get on to stop it, I fell, and it ran over me and continued on until a cherry tree stopped it," she says. "When I fell, the tractor had cleared Bobby, and he was laying in the garden with a lot more injuries than he got in Vietnam," she adds. A neighbor ran over, turned off the tractor, and called an ambulance. A helicopter took them to a hospital in Louisville, where she spent thirty-three days; he, twenty-five days.

Friendship, family, close ties bind this town together. Never was this more apparent than when the people rallied behind the Stumphs with a picnic, dance, auction, and various fund-raisers to help defray their hospital costs.

━━━━

Tom Raisor and Mozena Cecil were married a short time after he returned. "Bardstown hasn't changed a whole lot since the war," Mozena says. "It was a nice place to live then, it's still a nice place to live. If anything good did come out of the war, it brought us closer together, although we always were close. Now we're even closer.

"It's a good place to raise a family," she says. "I know that several families that moved away years ago have come back to live here.

"It's small. You know everyone, what they make, how many times they turn their lights on, how many times they turn them off, who they talked to when they were gone. Everybody knew everybody, and I liked that," she adds. "Tommy used to say, 'If I didn't know 'em, they didn't live in Nelson County.' "

"There really wasn't too much discussion about the war after I came home," Tom Raisor says. "I don't think anybody wanted to bring it up because it would bring back bad memories to those who were there.

"I do think there was a lot of bitterness, though," he says. "After the sacrifices that had been made, I don't think there would have been nearly as much bitterness if we had tried to win.

"I don't have any problem with why we were there. The only problem I have is the way we fought it," Raisor continues. "If you make a commitment to go to war, you gotta fight to win. We didn't.

"When I see something that reminds me of the war, I think about it. I still think about Jim Moore," he says.

Mozena Raisor remembers the war, too, the call-up of the Guard unit, and the party just before the men left for Texas.

"Tom danced with me that night for the first time. He hasn't danced with me since," she says.

━━━━━━

Roger Coffey, the young medic who, though badly wounded, patched up the men injured during the fighting that night, received the Silver Star for his action under fire. He lives in Louisville now and works for a firm that prints Sunday newspaper supplements and advertising. "I almost got married before I left, but I didn't want to leave a widow," he says, so he got married in November of 1969, a few weeks after he returned. His wife, Peggy, works for the Jefferson County school district.

"I don't even like to stop at a car wreck now. It makes me sick," he says. "I can if I have to, but I'd rather not."

Former Lt. Dan Doyle, who was the executive officer of Battery C the night it was attacked, lives in Richardson, Texas, and is sales manager for a firm involved in pollution abatement—"We build scrubbers for power plants."

Seriously wounded during the attack, he was first helicoptered to the hospital at Da Nang, then flown to a hospital just outside Tokyo, and finally sent to the hospital at Fort Knox. "The doctors wouldn't let me out of there because they said there were about four hundred pieces of metal in my body and they had only taken out about two-fifty," he says.

"However, I convinced them that if they let me out, I would go to a college near a Veterans Administration hospital so the doctors there could keep an eye on me. And they did, they let me out," he adds. So he went to the University of Cincinnati and received a master's degree in engineering.

Tom Eatmon, who was the commanding officer of Battery C when it was attacked but was on leave in Hawaii at that time, lives in Corbin, Kentucky. He is general superintendant with a railroad holding company. He is Doyle's brother-in-law.

Tom McClure, who trained the men in Battery C and was the unit's commanding officer when it was called to active duty and sent to Vietnam, still lives in the area and still works for the Salt River Rural Electric Cooperative Corporation in Bardstown, where he is an engineer. But he is no longer a member of the Kentucky National Guard.

———

Bertha Ford, the mother of Raymond Ford, the first young man from Bardstown to die in the war, passed away May 7, 1993, after a lengthy illness. She never supported the war, even at the beginning. Her daughter Brenda, who lives close by, seems to echo her mother's sentiments when she says: "I think about the war a lot. There are a lot of things around town to remind me. I often look at the monuments at the Courthouse Square. Even this house is a reminder. My mother had it built with Raymond's insurance money. There are family members of the others who were killed. You see them often on the street. I don't think the memories will ever go away. Never. I'm just glad the war is over."

———

Louis T. Blanford, who was badly wounded in both legs, and his wife, Linda, still live in St. Francis, Kentucky, about eighteen miles from Bardstown. He works at the General Electric plant in Louisville, she at a nursing home a short distance from where they live. They have five children.

———

Ronnie Hibbs, who was burned on the back and neck as he ran from Gun 1 toward a bunker, and his wife, Libby, live in Cox's Creek, Kentucky, about nine miles from Bardstown, as they have for many years. Libby has a beauty shop. Ronnie has a small trucking company. They keep their 1962 Ford Galaxie in perfect condition and cruise on Saturday nights. At present, he is restoring a 1929 Ford.

■■■

Larry Johnson, who crawled out of the wire bunker just before it was destroyed and who was probably the last person to talk with Ronnie Simpson and Ronnie McIlvoy before they were killed, still lives in Bardstown with his family.

■■■

Rebecca Crawford, whose husband, Air Force Capt. James J. Crawford, is the last person listed on the larger of the two monuments in Courthouse Square, still lives here, along with her daughter, Ellen, who is in college.

■■■

Several years ago, Kent Bischoff, who was the supply sergeant in Battery C, and his wife, Holly, went to Washington, D.C., to sightsee and visit the Vietnam Veterans Memorial. "Seeing thousands and thousands of names of the dead was very moving, very emotional," Holly remembers. But there was a large number of visitors there, and they were pressed for time, so Bischoff couldn't do what he had planned—get rubbings of the names of his friends who died at Fire Base Tomahawk. Early next morning, as they were about to leave for the Smithsonian, Bischoff said to his wife, "I've been there before. I think I'll go back to the wall."

"I understood what he was saying. He wanted some time alone there, without a lot of people watching," Holly says.

He took a taxi back to the wall, picked up several strips of paper—four inches wide by twenty-one inches long, with light carbon on one side—that are available there, located the names of his friends who were killed that night, then began to get rubbings of their names by placing the carbon side of the paper across a name, then rubbing a hard object, perhaps a pencil, across the name. Then the name began to appear, slowly, ethereally, on the paper.

Unbeknownst to Bischoff, a crowd began to gather. Then one woman ventured forward and asked, "Sir, you couldn't possibly know all those people."

"Yes, ma'am," he replied. "I surely do. I know every one of them personally."

"She couldn't get over that," he remembers.

"Perhaps the sacrifices were meaningless," Bischoff says. "As it turned out, we don't know. I hope they didn't die for nothing, but it almost looked like that when 1975 came and the whole thing fell apart."

Whenever Battery C, Fire Base Tomahawk, or the war in Vietnam is discussed around here, certain questions will rise. Perhaps Cheryl Simpson Lyvers, the daughter of Ronnie and Deanna Simpson, can explain this best.

"When I heard that someone was going to write about the guys that were over there and what had happened, I thought maybe now I'll find out how my dad really died. My mom to this day doesn't know the truth. There are three different stories. Just like Patsy Stone, nobody has told her exactly what happened to David Collins.

"It feels like the guys, including my father, who were killed are still in limbo, because nobody wants to talk about what was going on at the time, or five minutes before. What were each of them doing, and how did they die? All the mothers, wives, and kids of these men can only wonder. For me, I can't put him to rest until I know.

"My mom was told she couldn't see Dad because she couldn't recognize him. Another one said you could tell exactly who it was. If she could have seen him and decided for herself, she would have rested a lot easier. To be honest, with all the stories we've heard, how do we know it's him up in the graveyard?"

Of the Vietnam war, the attack on Fire Base Tomahawk, the intervening years, Charlene Chappel Hardt, daughter of Luther Chappel, who was killed that night, says: "There was a twenty year reunion that my mother, stepfather, me with my family, my sister with her family, attended. I felt like this helped me a great deal. It was painful, but at the same time a great help for me to talk with some of the men that knew my father and those who had spent so much time with him during his last months. After the reunion, I seemed to feel like I could finally, after twenty years, deal with this tragedy and put it all behind me.

"Sometime later, my neighbor called, very upset that her son was being sent to the Persian Gulf. It seemed to bring it all back again. Only this time, not only was there sadness in my heart for those men and their families, but for those who served in Vietnam and were criticized for doing so.

"I regret that I lost my father at such a young age. I regret the fact that he reenlisted to go to Vietnam. I regret the fact that there were so many things that I never got to share with him. I regret the fact that he never got to see my children. But most of all, I resent losing him.

"The Vietnam war still affects many of us in our everyday lives. You can never get rid of the feelings of not being able to understand why this happened to your family, or why you had to lose your father. To those of us who lost loved ones, it was not just another war or conflict. It was, and still is, a disruption of our lives, and some things will never be the same. There are nightmares and memories that still seem to haunt you after years of losing your natural father. But after several years of having a great stepfather, you even have nightmares of your father coming back and [your] having to pick between the two."

———

It's surprising that casualties were not greater than they were. Chaos and confusion during the attack were such that if you were not buttoned up in your gun, or in a bunker, almost surely you would have been shot, possibly even by friendly fire, because the hill was a mass of dark shapes running around on a very dark night.

"They trained well, and they fought well," remembers Tom Eatmon, the battery commander, who was on leave at the time of the battle. "The night they were hit, they accounted for themselves very well. If they didn't, they would have been annihilated. For a unit to fight like Charlie Battery did and not suffer horrendous casualties, well, that was a heroic thing."

I was told that, in the aftermath of the battle, paperwork began to creep through channels that would eventually result in Jim Moore's being posthumously awarded the Medal of Honor, but that the effort died on someone's desk. If so, this is not a fitting end when one is considered worthy of receiving this country's highest award for action above and beyond the call of duty.

———

David Unseld, who went to Vietnam with the battery but diffused out before the attack, expressed his thoughts in this poem he wrote while he was there:

Here I am in this wartorn land,
This place is known as Vietnam,
It's the coldest and darkest of nights
and the word is already down
That we'll have to fight,
then, I thought, God, how can it be
Will this war really make 'em free?
Then all at once I heard a terrifying sigh,
and there he was before my eyes.
He was my buddy from the other hill
I could tell you his name . . .
but you wouldn't know him still.
He was a guy like you and I,
and came here, sure, but not to die.
When I looked at his face to say a prayer,
I saw a trace of gray in his hair . . .

Oh, God, it must have scared him so
to see before him his own life unfold.
Friends and neighbors, I ask you please
When you pray to our Lord, our God,
Remember me, but especially guys like these.

Unseld began to write the poem the night that Reuben Simpson rolled down the hill and into the razor-sharp wire. "I was scared that night," Unseld remembers, "and when you're scared, you get close to God. Somebody did it for me. Somebody put those words in my head for me.

"I never wrote anything in my life other than that poem," he says.

The agony of Bardstown became a symbol of what was wrong across the land back then.

"I guess you'd have to characterize it [Vietnam], more or less, as one of the black marks on our country as far as military mistakes," says Elizabeth Spalding, former editor of the *Kentucky Standard*. When the war ended, public trust in the government to do the right thing most of the time had plummeted from a high of seventy-six percent in 1964 to a low of thirty-seven percent.

Vietnam will always be here, in Bardstown. It rears its head whenever you pass one of those who felt its effect, when you hear the distant booming of the big guns at Fort Knox.

Index

INDEX

INDEX

INDEX